**NEW DIRECTIONS
FOR CHILD
DEVELOPMENT**

Number 10 • 1980

NEW DIRECTIONS FOR CHILD DEVELOPMENT

A Quarterly Sourcebook
William Damon, Editor-in-Chief

Number 10, 1980

Children's Memory

Marion Perlmutter
Guest Editor

Jossey-Bass Inc., Publishers
San Francisco • Washington • London

CHILDREN'S MEMORY
New Directions for Child Development
Number 10, 1980
　　　Marion Perlmutter, Guest Editor

New Directions for Child Development (publication number
USPS 494-090) is published quarterly by Jossey-Bass Inc., Publishers.
Subscriptions are available at the regular rate for institutions,
libraries, and agencies of $30 for one year. Individuals may
subscribe at the special professional rate of $18 for one year.

Correspondence:
Subscriptions, single-issue orders, change of address notices,
undelivered copies, and other correspondence should be sent to
New Directions Subscriptions, Jossey-Bass Inc., Publishers,
433 California Street, San Francisco, California 94104.

Editorial correspondence should be sent to the Editor-in-Chief,
William Dàmon, Department of Psychology, Clark University,
Worcester, Massachusetts 01610.

Library of Congress Catalogue Card Number LC 80-81896
International Standard Serial Number ISSN 0195-2269
International Standard Book Number ISBN 87589-800-9

Cover design by Willi Baum
Manufactured in the United States of America

Contents

Editor's Notes

Many investigators of human cognition are becoming sensitive to naturalistic approaches. This trend is evident in shifts in the phenomena being investigated as well as in changes in the models and methods that are employed. These new directions have been fostered by several factors. First, researchers are increasingly required to be "accountable" for their work. It presently seems easier to justify the study of ecologically valid phenomena than more traditionally investigated phenomena. Second, there seems to be a conceptual shift in assumptions about the nature of human behavior. While it was assumed previously that *general* laws of behavior were discoverable, more and more it is believed that only more *specific* laws apply. These changing views have led to a greater emphasis on which phenomena to investigate as well as on the context in which they should be investigated. A third related factor contributing to interest in naturalistic approaches has been the recent advancement, in several related fields, of a sociobiological model for behavior. Finally, there are a number of practical reasons for adopting a naturalistic approach. While standard laboratory methodologies permit controlled collection of data that are relatively easy to analyze, these methodologies appear less than optimal for assessing the skills of some subjects. This dilemma is especially apparent with subjects at the extremes of the life span, which probably explains why investigators of very young children have been especially receptive to naturalistic approaches.

The present volume is devoted to reports of research in which this paradigmatic shift is evident. The purpose of this presentation is to provide a preliminary account of progress that may have resulted from increased sensitivity to ecological validity and naturalistic perspectives on human cognition and behavior. In particular it is hoped that the contrasts of questions that have been asked and techniques that have been adopted will prove useful in evaluating the potential of a naturalistic approach, as well as in pointing to fruitful directions for the future.

The focus of all of the research in this volume is children's memory. This topic has received relatively extensive experimental attention in the last decade or two, and there is now considerable understanding of how children perform on laboratory memory tasks and how this performance improves with age. However, it is less clear whether much has been learned about how children typically use their past experiences in dealing with the present and in planning for the future. It is hoped that the research presented here begins to address these important issues.

The research, carried out in relatively naturalistic situations, differed in terms of subjects' ages, types of memory, contexts of the investigations, and degree of control and manipulation. One of the studies included infants under one year of age (Ashmead and Perlmutter), some involved toddlers between one-and-one-half and three (DeLoache; Wellman and Somerville), and others were restricted to older preschool children, three and four years of age (Ratner; Todd and Perlmutter; Nelson and Ross). More important differences among the studies involved the questions that were addressed. Judy DeLoache was interested specifically in spatial memory, as were Henry Wellman and Susan Somerville, and to some extent Daniel Ashmead and Marion Perlmutter. In addition, Wellman and Somerville also pursued children's memory of routines. On the other hand, some investigators were more interested in describing the range of everyday memory use by young children (Ashmead and Perlmutter) and everyday memory demands placed on them (Ratner). Several investigators relied on conversational formats to uncover children's everyday use of memory knowledge (Ratner; Todd and Perlmutter; Nelson and Ross). In two studies there was also an attempt to compare children's everyday use of memory with their performance on more standard experimental tasks (Ratner; Todd and Perlmutter). The contexts of the research ranged from the laboratory to preschools and play yards (Wellman and Somerville) as well as homes (Ashmead and Perlmutter; Ratner; Todd and Perlmutter). In addition, in some studies there was fairly extensive reliance on control and manipulation (DeLoache; Wellman and Somerville), in others there was less direction by the experimenters (Todd and Perlmutter; Nelson and Ross), and in two of the investigations there was almost total reliance on observations of ongoing behavior (Ashmead and Perlmutter; Ratner).

All of these authors acknowledged certain limitations in their approach, and many appear to have posed more questions than they definitively resolved. Still, it seems that this research perspective may highlight important domains for investigation that have been too long ignored. While the research discussed in the pages that follow is just in its beginning stages, it seems to hold much promise.

Marion Perlmutter
Guest Editor

Marion Perlmutter is an associate professor at the University of Minnesota's Institute of Child Development.

Research is reported that was aimed at identifying a fuller range of
infant memory behavior than was previously available.

Infant Memory in Everyday Life

Daniel H. Ashmead
Marion Perlmutter

Most research on infant memory has focused on visual recognition (see Cohen and Gelber, 1975; Werner and Perlmutter, 1979). While some processes involved in such memory are beginning to be well understood (for example, the use of "prototypical" information in facial recognition (Strauss, 1979), a portrayal of the full range of infant memory abilities has not yet emerged. The purpose of the present study was to identify a fuller range of infant memory behavior. For reasons discussed below, laboratory methodologies did not seem most appropriate for this task. Therefore, parents were asked to keep diaries of their infants' everyday memory behavior.

The general issue of interest, how prior experience influences ongoing behavior, is common to several traditions of research on infants, including learning theory (Lipsitt, 1970), sensorimotor intelligence (Piaget, 1952, 1954), visual information processing (Cohen and Gelber, 1975), speech act theory (Bates, 1976), and language comprehension (Huttenlocher, 1974). While many of the observations reported could be interpreted in terms of these

The authors would like to express their appreciation to the families who participated so enthusiastically in this study, and to Celia Brownell, John Cavanaugh, Jayne Grady, Jeffrey Lockman, Donna Marget, Chris Todd, and Carol Revermann for their help and suggestions. The research was supported by a NICHHD (No. HD11776) grant to Marion Perlmutter.

traditions, for present purposes they were interpreted in terms of memory constructs. Five main questions were addressed: What is the content of infants' everyday memory? What is the nature of contextual support for it? Are there differences in infants' use of memory for relatively permanent versus temporary properties of the world (for example, locations of stationary versus moveable objects)? What is the role of active participation (as opposed to more passive registration of information) in infants' memory? Are there differences in infants' memory of person- versus object-related situations?

Laboratory methodologies have facilitated an understanding of infant memory; however, such methodologies have some important limitations, particularly for older infants. First, infants' exposure to stimuli is unrelated to their ongoing activity outside of the specific experimental task. Second, the types of stimuli and their history of exposure are constrained much more than in infants' everyday lives (for example, most experiments involve repeated exposure to pictures over a period of less than one-half hour). Third, the range of infant behaviors indicative of memory is small (for example, visual fixation, operant sucking), and inferences are usually only whether or not some memory-based discrimination was made. Because of these limitations, an observational methodology was used.

To our knowledge there have been two previous observational studies of infant memory, Hurlock and Schwartz (1932) and Fox, Kagan, and Weiskopf (1979). Hurlock and Schwartz reviewed the records of thirty-six late nineteenth and early twentieth century "baby biographers." Examples of memory behavior observed during the first year of life included visual recognition of people, social games with caregivers, and daily routines such as feeding. Hurlock and Schwartz's conclusion about memory during the first year was that its predominant feature is visual recognition. This conclusion is consistent with recent experimental research on infants' memory early in the first year, but is somewhat at odds with the findings of the Fox *et al.* study, as well as those of the present study. To anticipate, in both of these more recent studies, which focused on the second half of the first year, there has been evidence of memory abilities besides recognition. This discrepancy may have arisen because Hurlock and Schwartz's conclusions were based on the first year as a whole. Indeed, their conclusions about the second year were that there was more memory for actions, less of a requirement of perceptual presence of the stimulus, and greater tolerance of delay. Thus, Hurlock and Schwartz simply may have marked the transition as occurring slightly later than has been observed in subsequent studies.

Fox and others (1979) studied eight infants longitudinally from five to fourteen months, repeatedly administering a set of memory tasks. These tasks included comparison of familar and novel toys, object permanence, hiding of objects, picture recognition, and reactions to the presence of unfamiliar adults and separation from caregivers. Since these memory situations involved short time periods and small spaces, and did not include situations with which the infants had repeated experiences, they are relevant primarily to infants' memory of short-term exposure to novel situations. In general, results suggested that late in the first year there is an increasing tolerance for delay and interference, as well as the beginning of representational abilities. The former trend is consistent with the experimental literature on infant recognition memory (see Werner and Perlmutter, 1979). The latter trend generally is consistent with Piaget's views of the development of representation (Piaget, 1962; Piaget and Inhelder, 1973), although Piaget did not find much evidence of representation until after the first year. Thus, previous studies have suggested that new memory abilities, such as representation, emerge late in the first year.

Method

A parental diary method was used for the present study. This methodology enabled behavioral episodes to be interpreted in their long-term, natural context, and optimized the likelihood of observing infrequent, unpredictable episodes. The final sample consisted of eleven infants in three age groups, seven-, nine-, and eleven-month-olds (at the beginning of the six-week study). Within each age-group, sex and sibling status (only child versus one older sibling) were counter-balanced, except that there was only one seven-month-old girl (an only child). All of the families resided in lower- to middle-class neighborhoods.

Families made daily observations in a diary for six weeks. During an initial home visit the nature of infant memory was discussed and the unique observational opportunities of parents were pointed out. Parents were asked to consider "any behavior that utilizes past experience." In addition, the recognition/recall distinction was discussed, and parents were asked to look especially for "the ability to remember past experiences outside of their original context." They were provided with written examples of three memory episodes. These were an infant: (1) getting a familiar out-of-sight toy, upon verbal request from a parent; (2) being excited upon seeing his grandfather (this was an example of recognition); and (3) happening upon a "stacker" toy and going to get another part of it. In addition to these examples, others were discussed, particularly ones that parents volunteered about their own infants.

Parents were given printed diary forms and were asked to make entries every day, even if it was just to say, "nothing observed," or "no time." They were phoned about once a week in order to discuss specific observations they had made. A final visit occurred after the sixth week. Observations were made by both parents in five of the families, only by the mother in another five, and only by the father in one.

Coding and Analysis

A total of 298 observations were collected, or about twenty-seven per family (range = seven to forty-two). The first task was to screen episodes in order to reject those that were uncodable because of insufficient detail. A codable memory episode was defined as any observation in which specific behavior was described and in which there was evidence of utilization of past experience by the infant. Of the 298 observations, 239 were codable (80 percent).

If an episode was considered appropriate for coding, it was necessary to decide which aspect of it to focus upon. Most of the episodes were straightforward in this respect. This episode of a seven-month-old (whose name has been changed, as have all names in the chapter) is an example:

> My husband called from work and I let him talk to Rob. He looked puzzled for a while and then he turned and looked at the door. Rob thought of the only time he hears his dad's voice when he knows Dad isn't home is when his dad just got home. He heard his dad's voice and based on past experiences, he reasoned that his dad must be home, so he looked at the door.

Coding of this episode focused on the possible association of the father's voice with the act of the father entering the door (although, of course, the infant did not necessarily make the series of inferences suggested by the mother).

The following episode involving an eleven-month-old is less straightforward:

> Louise is crying, at my knee, while I'm drinking coffee on the couch, because she wants what's in the cup. Her father called from behind her, "Louise, where is your baby? Go find your baby." (Baby is the name for her doll.) She grabbed the toy baby bottle that was on the couch and headed right for the doll that was in the dining room. She came back in the living room and played with the doll for five minutes. This is one of the rare times we've been able to distract her from something verbally; usually it's a matter of physically redirecting her actions.

It was possible to focus upon the infant's : (1) use of crying as a means for getting food; (2) knowledge of "baby" as a referent for the doll; (3) association of the bottle with the doll (she had demonstrated this on previous occasions as well); (4) location of the doll; or, (5) participation in the request-fetch game with her parents. A criterion of focusing on the aspect of the episode that most seemed to incorporate other aspects was chosen. Thus, the focus of this example was the request-fetch game; it seemed to subsume all but the first type of knowledge mentioned above (the first was considered an ancillary point to this observation). By similar analyses, the focal points of each of the codable episodes were determined.

Once the focal points of the episodes were determined, they were classified into one of five mutually exclusive categories based on the knowledge content shown by the infant. There was 94 percent inter-rater agreement for this categorization, which is described below.

Perceptual Attributes of Objects or People. This category typ‍‍
involved an infant noticing minor changes in the visual characteristics or
something or someone, or recognizing people as familiar. An example was an
infant being wary of her grandmother the first time she saw her wearing sun-
glasses.

Functional Attributes of Objects or People. The focus here was on
the infant's knowledge of some attribute of an object or person that was not
immediately perceptible. This type of knowledge could be revealed by the
infant's action. Many such episodes involved "appropriate" play with toys, as
in this example involving a seven-month-old:

> Anne was offered a four-inch cloth cube — a favorite toy. Upon
> grasping it she immediately began shaking it to hear a tinkle inside the
> cube. Anne would normally mouth an object first. In this case she
> passed by this examination, remembering that a noise is produced by
> shaking the cloth object.

Locations of Objects or People. In many episodes the most salient
feature was knowledge of locations. These are discussed in detail below.

Initiative Social Interaction. A social interaction was defined as any
sequence of behavior in which two or more people were influenced directly by
each other's behavior. Infants were presumed to play an initiating role if they
were first to engage the other persons, or if they were first to take part in a significant change in the course of the interaction. An example of the latter was
the following mealtime interaction of an eleven-month-old:

> Albert eating lunch. Handed Dorine (babysitter) his glass.
> Dorine saw it was empty and filled it. He did the same for me several
> days ago. Twice during one meal he handed me his glass. Each time it
> was empty. Each time I filled it.

Responsive Social Interaction. This kind of knowledge was similar to
that included in the social initiation category, except that the infant neither
initiated the interaction nor brought about a significant shift in it. An example
is this peek-a-boo episode of a nine-month-old:

> Wednesday evening. Greg is playing in his high chair after eat-
> ing supper. I say "peek-a-boo" and Greg holds his bib in front of his
> face.

Findings

Content of Memory. The percentage of episodes involving each type
of knowledge is shown for each age group in Figure 1. Every infant demonstrated each type of knowledge. Moreover, there appeared to be an age-related

Figure 1. Mean Percentage of Each Age Group's Episodes That Demonstrated Each Type of Knowledge

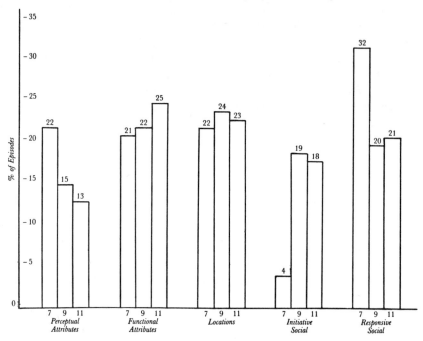

trend toward more initiation of social interactions, especially between seven and nine months.

Support for Memory. Most memory that involved perceptual support was demonstrated by an emotional response of familiarity (such as smiling or crying) or a surprise reaction. The types of information that elicited such recognition included people, objects, and names. The mean number of these types of episodes is shown in Table 1. No age changes were apparent.

Infants also are likely to possess some retrieval processes. These skills would be reflected in infants' utilization of information not available in immediate perception. The most direct evidence of such skills was infants' knowledge of location of objects and people. While the findings on memory for locations will be presented in detail in the next section, it should be noted that virtually all of the location episodes involved knowledge of things that were not perceptually available. That is, search behavior was organized around objects and people that were temporally and spatially remote. Thus, the infants seemed to have some representational abilities.

Retrieval skills also appeared in infants' initiation of social interactions. Moreover, there was an age increase in such episodes, that may be seen in Figure 1. An analysis of the infant-initiated social interactions indicated that the age change consisted largely of an increase in initiating behaviors that

Table 1. Mean Number of Episodes Involving Recognition of People, Physical Objects, or Names for Each Age Group

Age	People	Objects	Names
7 months	1.67	3.33	.33
9 months	1.75	1.25	.25
11 months	.50	1.50	.50

could be described as communicative. The definition of *communicative* was that it was apparent that the infant had some goal that the other person could help attain. Thus, for an episode to be considered communicative, it had to be reasonably clear to the other person what the infant wanted, and the infant had to show some evidence of being "satisfied" when the goal was attained. An example may be seen in the following episode:

> I've been trying to teach Louise to kiss by kissing her and her doll. Louise came up to me with her doll and was holding it up to me. She was babbling something, then she got a little upset. I took the doll and gave it a kiss then gave it back to her and she gave the doll a kiss, too.

It is likely that the older infants expected other people to behave in certain ways on the basis of the infant's own behavior (for example, "expecting" the mother to kiss the doll). While memory seems necessary for such an expectation, the exact relationship between the expectation and memory processes is obscure. Piaget and Inhelder (1973) recognized this problem when they discussed infants' "anticipation" of events. It might be that "memory per se" plays an important role early during the acquisition of communicative behaviors, such as the example above. Later on, behaviors might be more generalized. Thus, Louise at first might have remembered the specific effect of her offering the doll (that is, that her mother kissed it). Later, she might have developed a more general ability to obtain help from her mother. A thorough discussion of this issue is beyond the scope of this chapter. However, it should be noted that late in the first year infants do seem to become better able to use knowledge to initiate social interactions, regardless of how this use is interpreted.

Temporary Versus Permanent Locations. The question of whether infants remember temporary and permanent properties of the world was addressed most directly by episodes involving memory for location. Younger infants seemed to remember primarily the locations of objects with permanent locations, whereas older infants remembered temporary locations as well. Examples of permanent locations include the cupboard where cereal is kept, the telephone, and the potato bin. Temporary locations were divided into two categories, inanimate objects (such as toys and small household items) and animate things (such as people and pets). Table 2 contains the mean number

Table 2. Mean Number of Episodes Involving Permanent and
Temporary Locations for Each Age Group

Age	Permanent Location	Temporary Location			Proportion of Temporary Locations
		Total	Animate	Inanimate	
7 months	4.33	1.00	.33	.67	.19
9 months	2.75	2.25	1.75	.50	.45
11 months	2.0	1.25	.25	1.00	.38

of each type of location episode for each age group. As may be seen, the nine- and eleven-month-olds had more episodes of memory for temporary locations than the seven-month-olds.

There were two interesting qualitative components to this transition. The first concerned locations of people. Each of the nine-month-olds commonly "searched" for a parent, for example, in the parent's bedroom. Moreover, the infants seemed to search systematically through several rooms. That is, they searched all around each room and did not repeat looking in a room they already had been to. Parents of the eleven-month-olds also reported this behavior, but they believed that it had been going on for a long time and so did not make many diary entries about it. In contrast, the seven-month-olds, even when they were adept at crawling, did not show any evidence that they expected people to be in certain locations. The only such instance reported for a seven-month-old involved his "discovery" of his mother as she slept late one morning and then repeated returns to the bedroom to look at the bed. Thus, unlike the older infants, the seven-month-olds did not seem to know about the range of possible locations of people and did not take into account the last location in which the person was seen.

The second qualitative transition in infant's memory for locations involved memories over fairly long periods of time for locations of objects that had been used and then left. Here is an example involving an eleven-month-old:

> Louise had been playing with a small doll bottle. She let it go on the floor and it rolled partially under the refrigerator. She went in her room and was playing for fifteen to twenty minutes when she found her doll and went back to where she had left her bottle, picked it up, and went back to her room.

This sort of episode, where infants seemed to remember where they had left things, was observed only in eleven-month-olds. It appeared that temporary locations of objects were not as salient for seven- and nine-month-olds as for eleven-month-olds. Although older infants did not have extensive experience with temporary locations, they seemed to register the locations and had them available for at least a few hours. This age trend toward better use of memory of temporary locations, therefore, might involve a dissociation of spatial location information from other knowledge about objects (for example, knowledge about the infant's own action with respect to the object). Most permanent locations were associated with particular behavior patterns, such as the cereal cupboard being associated with requesting food and eating, or the utensil cupboard being associated with playing with pots and pans. In such cases the spatial location information may have been undifferentiated with respect to infants' actions. Temporary locations, on the other hand, were not as uniquely associated with infants' actions. Thus, memory for an object's temporary location would need to be dissociated from memory for any action uniquely related to the object.

This dissociation interpretation is related to Piaget's (1954) work on the development of the object concept. At the end of Piaget's fourth stage of the object concept, if infants have seen an object moved from location A to location B, they will search correctly at B even though they are used to finding the object at A. At the end of the fifth stage, they will successfully follow multiple visible displacements, from A to B to C. Bremner and Bryant (1977) provided evidence that, at least at nine months of age, errors on such object-concept tasks are due to the use of a learned response (reaching to one of two hiding places) in situations where it is no longer appropriate. That is, the response seems to be remembered, but it is not dissociated from the spatial location. In a sense, the eleven-month-olds in the present sample were solving a task like the fourth or fifth stage object-concept tasks (depending upon how many "displacements" of the object the infant had made). That is, they searched where they had last seen the object.

Both the Piagetian object-concept tasks and the search behavior of the eleven-month-olds in this sample can be interpreted in terms of a dissociation between an object's location and the infant's action with respect to the object. Huttenlocher's (1974) observations of infants' responses to verbal requests to fetch objects provide further support for this dissociation model. In a study of language comprehension in four children from ten to eighteen months old, she found the following sequence of search behaviors in response to verbal requests for objects: (1) only at locations within an immediate perceptual space; (2) for objects with permanent locations; and (3) for objects with temporary locations. Recall that in the present study seven- and nine-month-olds searched for objects with permanent locations, but only eleven-month-olds searched at temporary locations. Whereas the infants in Huttenlocher's sample were not searching at temporary locations upon verbal request, the infants in the present sample *were* searching at temporary locations at an *earlier* age, apparently in response to more endogenous stimulation. It is possible that infants have knowledge of temporary locations that is evidenced when searching on their own, but may not be adept at retrieving it in the service of requests. It is an intriguing possibility that searching for something upon verbal request is an action that at first cannot be dissociated from object location.

If this is true, then the *memory* problem is not so much whether infants can register temporary locations of objects, but rather, how this information can be integrated with the infant's ongoing behavior.

So far infants' search for objects and the possible dissociation of knowledge about object location from knowledge about the infant's action on the object have been discussed. Next, a different aspect of infants' memory for locations, their search for persons, is considered. Recall that at nine and eleven months infants commonly went throughout the house systematically looking for a particular person. On the surface, this behavior bears some relation to the sixth stage of Piaget's object concept. At the end of this stage, invisible displacements of an object are registered by infants. However, infants' search for persons may be quite different than their search for objects. For example, in the stage-six task, infants see the displacement activity, although they do not see the object itself during the displacement. In searching for people, infants typically do not have any immediate basis for knowing where the person has gone. Rather, they may have searched systematically among a variety of likely locations (bedroom, kitchen, and so on). A given location may have been more or less likely depending upon contextual circumstances (for example, some infants went to their parents' bedroom in the morning if one parent was not up yet). Infants' search for people may reflect an awareness that people move about in patterns that are only partially predictable from one's own observations of their movements. This point is consistent with Bell's (1970) finding of object permanence for animate objects before inanimate ones. If infants have such knowledge about people, then a memory problem would be to distinguish between the last place a person was seen and the likely location of the person based on the intervening context. Episodes such as searching for a parent in her bedroom in the morning suggest that infants are sensitive to this contextual information.

Active Experience. The findings most relevant to the role of active experience in memory involve the role of locomotion in the development of spatial knowledge. It is apparent from observations such as an infant's becoming excited when a parent opens the cupboard where cookies are kept that infants remember the locations of some things even without having had the experience of moving to them. However, such episodes involve locations within a perceptual space. That is, the infant's knowledge is that an object is *contained* within something that the infant can see. It might be that the active experience of moving to locations is necessary to develop spatial memory for larger-scale environments, such as a house. With this possibility in mind, we were interested when two of the three seven-month-olds began to crawl during the study. Of interest was whether the infants would locomote to out-of-sight locations very soon after they acquired the ability to crawl or creep. Such an occurrence would support the position that extensive locomotion experience per se is not necessary for the integration of a large-scale space. Both families were asked to observe their infants carefully during this time, and both reported that it was not until several days after the infants could locomote fairly well that they went to out-of-sight locations with any indication of deliberateness. The following episodes indicate what the infants did a few days after learning to crawl:

> John just began true crawling on hands and knees several days ago. (He had been able to creep for a while, but could not go in one direction for more than a few feet.) On the same day he discovered the hallway which leads to the bathroom and laundry room. He now remembers where those rooms are and responds with excitement as he crawls towards them.
>
> Trying to change Anne's diaper and dress her in A.M. on changing table. She immediately turns over and crawls to top edge of table and reaches over edge several times. Today I had picked up the pink lotion so it wasn't where she expected it to be. Anne paused, looked back and forth and looked at me puzzled. Her eyes brightened when she saw the bottle — immediately took it from me.

While these two infants did not show evidence of memory for distant locations *immediately* after they began to locomote, their spatial location memory seemed quite accurate within only a few days. It is possible that they acquired specific memories for locations on the basis of very limited active locomotion experience. On the other hand, it seems likely that their extensive passive experience with the locations (being carried around) also afforded them spatial information. If this was true, perhaps the knowledge was not used immediately because they were not yet adept enough at locomoting in a large space. Another possibility, related to the dissociation interpretation of infants' search discussed earlier, is that they knew the spatial layout of the house quite well, but could not use it immediately for locomotion behavior.

An interesting coincidence relating to these considerations occurred with one of the infants. John started to creep and crawl while he and his family were on vacation in another city. When the family returned home, John's parents did not believe that he knew his way around their house (that is, he did not crawl to out-of-sight locations in an uninterrupted manner, even though he had been doing so at the other house during the vaction). Thus, John's only knowledge about the layout of the home was based on prior passive experience, and there did not seem to be evidence of benefits from such passive experience. Of course, this finding is complicated by the confound of delay and interference of being in a different house for two weeks.

Objects Versus People. It has been reported already that infants searched at variable locations for people before they did so for objects. Now another aspect of infants' knowledge in social and nonsocial domains is considered, that of causal relations (Piaget, 1954). To anticipate, generally it was found that causal relations were more advanced in the social than in the nonsocial domain. This finding is germane to a consideration of memory development in at least two respects. First, it suggests that social behavior as well as object behavior must be considered in a thorough description of early memory use. Second, and more important theoretically, memory abilities used in understanding causal relations may develop first with respect to social behavior and later with respect to physical causality. It is possible, for example, that social figures help infants to understand causal relations by easing the memory demands in the situation. In contrast, infants may receive little such assistance in the understanding of physical causality.

Piaget has suggested a developmental sequence of understanding causal relations. First, infants' acts do not produce consistent effects external to their own bodies. Then, infants are aware of external effects, but only in terms of the consequences of their own actions. Finally, infants are aware of causal influence independent of themselves as objects as well as agents of causal influences. Out of the fifty-seven episodes demonstrating knowledge of functional attributes, fifty-three appeared to involve the second, egocentric type of causal relation. Examples of this egocentric type of causal understanding included opening and closing doors, pulling a balloon by a string, and making toys produce sounds. The following episode is an example from a ten-month-old who frequently played with doors:

> John on floor in kitchen. I have secured some of the cupboards with rubber bands so that John can't get into them. Today he began manipulating the edges of the cupboard doors which are banded shut in an attempt to open them. (The knobs are too high for him to pull. Other cupboards he has opened have been left ajar.) I think he knows that this is a *door* which leads to something interesting and is trying his new skill of manipulating doors.

As with most of Piaget's examples, all of the present fifty-three episodes of egocentric causal understanding involved physical relationships (such as opening a door). The remaining three observations fit the criterion of the third type of causality, awareness of causal influences independent of one's own actions, but all involved social figures. For example:

> The telephone rang and Louise and I were in the living room. Louise dropped what she was doing and headed as fast as she could toward the kitchen and pulled on the phone cord. A lot of times when the phone rings I'll bring Louise with me to answer it. This is the first time she responded to the ringing like this.

It seems that the overwhelming majority of episodes demonstrating knowledge of functional attributes involved egocentric causality. These episodes entailed physical relationships rather than social ones. It will be seen later than the picture was quite different for the social domain.

Infants seemed to know that other people could act as agents in social interactions, that is, that others acted independently but nonetheless in a manner related to the infants' actions. Of the ninety-two episodes of social interaction, sixty-three involved some kind of knowledge of another person as a social agent. Sometimes infants appeared to anticipate aversive or positive interactions with another person. For example:

> John has his first cold and has had to have his nose wiped repeatedly, which he dislikes. After his meal, I usually use a washcloth to wash his hands, then his face. As soon as I began to wash his hands, he responded by pulling his hands to his face and turning his face away from me.

Infants also seemed to know about the prohibition of certain activities, and seemed aware of contingencies, such that they would do something only if the "enforcer" was not looking at them. For example:

> The broom closet which holds our garbage cans is off limits to John. We have not always shut this door tightly and John always seizes the opportunity to scramble over there and open the door to inspect things if we leave the door ajar. We have always caught him and removed him before any damage is done. Today, I left the door ajar and John began moving toward it. This time, however, he was not scrambling but "sneaking," moving very slowly and eyeing me after each movement. It seemed as if he was waiting to see if I would notice him.

Among the nine- and eleven-month-olds there were several episodes in which the infants not only seemed aware of the parents as enforcers, but also seemed to enjoy "getting caught." Perhaps the confirmation of their expectation about the parents' reactions was enjoyable. There also were a number of social games in which infants seemed to have some knowledge about the roles of other people. For example, in the following episode the infant seemed to have a fairly abstract conception of the uncle's role in peek-a-boo game:

> Elinor played a long game of peek-a-boo with her uncle. Whenever he began slowing his responses, Elinor would change the rules. She went from behind the couch, to behind a table, to moving her whole body up and down behind a small chest.

The rule seemed to be that Elinor should disappear from her uncle's sight. One could argue that she simply made the uncle disappear from her own sight, but she did not do this by less elaborate means, such as closing her eyes or covering her face.

In these examples, infants' knowledge of social causality was less ego-centric than in the episodes involving physical causality. That is, there seemed to be some awareness of others as agents. Nonetheless, for the most part the episodes showing knowledge of social causality involved some contingency of the social figure's behavior on that of the infant. This interdependence may partially explain infants' earlier development of causality in the social than in the nonsocial domain. That is, since physical causal forces do not depend on the infant's behavior to the extent that social ones do, physical causes may be less salient. This possibility is related to the speculation made at the beginning of this section that social figures ease the memory demands placed on infants. For example, parents adjusted their own roles in peek-a-boo games to compensate for the infant's apparent "rules" (Bruner and Sherwood, 1976, have investigated this game in detail). Also, parents often provided some clues that they were about to get the infant a snack, such as placing the infant in a high chair or saying the names of foods. This behavior could have made the parent's role in getting the food and giving it to the infant more salient. In conclusion, there may be a mutual influence between memory abilities and knowledge of causal relations during early development.

Summary

A few general points will serve to summarize the present findings. First, observational data on infants collected by their parents can provide a feasible and informative way of increasing knowledge of early memory development, and this approach may be vital to an understanding of early cognitive development. For example, several age-related changes in memory were differentially evident in social and nonsocial situations. Therefore, many important transitions may not be captured adequately in traditional laboratory tests of memory, which are typically almost devoid of social stimuli. Second, interesting findings emerged concerning several more specific issues. In particular, these naturalistic observations provided information that is relevant to the context of infants' memory, the role of active experience in infants' memory, and the relationship between infants' specific memories and general knowledge structures about information in social and nonsocial domains.

One aspect of the context of infants' memory that was considered concerned its elicitors. The findings on spatial locations indicated that infants are not dependent entirely on perceptual information in their use of memory. They seem to have some representational abilities as well. Also, infants commonly initiated social interactions by nine months, indicating that they were not wholly reliant on others to provide cues for interactions.

A second aspect of the problem of context considered was the relationship between remembered information and infant's behavior with respect to that information. It was suggested that when infants use a relatively new behavioral search pattern they do not dissociate their own behavior from the location of the target object. Thus, at first they are able to use the behavior only for objects with permanent locations, since in those cases there is no need to dissociate their behavior from the location. Later, they are able to search at variable locations. Whereas in this study infants less than a year searched at temporary locations when they were "reminded" of the object in the course of some ongoing activity, in Huttenlocher's (1974) study infants older than a year did not search at temporary locations upon verbal request from an adult. Thus, even if information is registered by the infant, it may not be used for all types of behavior.

A third aspect of context that was considered was the relationship between remembered information and other knowledge infants have about a situation. For example, it is generally efficient to search for an object where it was seen last, but more efficient to search for a person based on broader contextual information (such as time of day). Searching for a person therefore represents a potential conflict between specific memory of where the person was last seen and general knowledge of where the person might be. By nine months, infants seemed to be able to take contextual information into account, and by eleven months they seemed to rely more on the latter source of information. Thus, an important aspect of the development of memory abilities may be knowing when to ignore specific remembrances.

The role of active experience in memory was also considered. The extent to which infants remember spatial layouts who began to crawl during the study are only suggestive, since passive experience and the dissociation of memory for a spatial layout from the behavior that was originally associated with it were confounded. There are, however, possible experiments that could separate these issues.

A final concern was memory for objects versus memory for people. The issue of how specific memory for social and nonsocial information relates to more general knowledge structures was raised. While it is obvious that knowledge structures impose fundamental constraints on what can be remembered, the opposite relationship holds as well. Memory demands placed on infants may be reduced in social situations relative to nonsocial situations, and this fact may affect the development of knowledge of causality in social and nonsocial domains.

In summary, the issues raised here are not simple, and most of the findings warrant more systematic investigation. However, the findings demonstrate a broad range of memory skills that infants use in everyday life. It appears that observational data on infants collected by their parents can provide a feasible and informative way of increasing our knowledge of early memory development.

References

Bates, E. *Language and Context: The Acquisition of Pragmatics.* New York: Academic Press, 1976.

Bell, S. "The Development of the Concept of Object as Related to Infant Mother Attachment." *Child Development,* 1970, *41,* 291–313.

Bremner, J. G., and Bryant, P. E. "Place Versus Response as the Basis of Spatial Errors Made by Young Infants." *Journal of Experimental Child Psychology*, 1977, *23*, 162–171.

Bruner, J. S., and Sherwood, V. "Peek-a-Boo and the Learning of Rule Structures." In J. S. Bruner, A. Jolly, and K. Sylva (Eds.), *Play — Its Role in Development and Evolution*. New York: Basic Books, 1976.

Cohen, L. B., and Gelber, E. R. "Infant Visual Memory." In L. B. Cohen and P. Salapatek (Eds.), *Infant Perception: From Sensation to Cognition*. Vol. 1: *Basic Visual Processes*. New York: Academic Press, 1975.

Fox, N., Kagan, J., and Weiskopf, S. "The Growth of Memory During Infancy." *Genetic Psychology Monographs*, 1979, *99*, 91–130.

Hurlock, E. B., and Schwartz, R. "Biographical Records of Memory in Preschool Children." *Child Development*, 1932, *3*, 230–239.

Huttenlocher, J. "The Origins of Language in Comprehension." In R. L. Solso (Ed.), *Theories in Cognitive Psychology: The Loyola Symposium*. Hillsdale, N.J.: Erlbaum, 1974.

Lipsitt, L. P. "The Experiential Origins of Human Behavior." In L. Goulet and P. Baltes (Eds.), *Life-Span Developmental Psychology: Research and Theory*. New York: Academic Press, 1970.

Piaget, J. *The Origins of Intelligence in Children*. New York: International Universities Press, 1952.

Piaget, J. *The Construction of Reality in the Child*. New York: Basic Books, 1954.

Piaget, J. *Play, Dreams, and Imitation in Childhood*. New York: Norton, 1962.

Piaget, J., and Inhelder, B. *Memory and Intelligence*. New York: Basic Books, 1973.

Strauss, M. S. "Abstraction of Prototypical Information by Adults and Ten-Month-Old Infants." *Journal of Experimental Psychology: Human Learning and Memory*, 1979, *5*, 618–632.

Werner, J. S., and Perlmutter, M. "Development of Visual Memory in Infants." In H. W. Reese and L. P. Lipsitt (Eds.), *Advances in Child Development and Behavior*. Vol. 14. New York: Academic Press, 1979.

Daniel H. Ashmead is a graduate student at the University of Minnesota's Institute of Child Development, where he has held NSF and Eva O. Miller graduate fellowships since receiving his bachelor's degree from Brown University in 1976.

Marion Perlmutter is an associate professor at the University of Minnesota's Institute of Child Development, where she has been on the faculty since receiving her Ph.D. degree in Psychology at the University of Massachusetts in 1976.

This chapter describes research on very young children's memory for location that was aimed at accurately assessing the memorial competence of young children.

Naturalistic Studies of Memory for Object Location in Very Young Children

Judy S. DeLoache

Gelman (1978) has pointed out that developmental psychologists have tended to view the young child as cognitively inept. In contrast, any parents will gladly regale any available listeners with numerous accounts of the impressive memory performance of their young children. For example, a friend related that she had searched in vain for the tiny yellow plastic piece to a toy that had been missing for days. In desperation, she asked her two-year-old if he knew where it was. Much to her surprise, he led her directly to it. My own son at twenty-one months, on taking his second walk down a street more than a week after an earlier trip there, returned to the exact spot where he had encountered his first snail and tried diligently to find it again.

Anecdotal accounts such as these cannot be used as data. Nonetheless, we should not ignore them completely. Such informal reports can be used to a

This research was supported by grant from NICHHD (No. HD05951). Thanks to Kay Bussey, Gerald Clore, Sophia Cohen, and Susan Sugarman for their helpful comments on an earlier version of this chapter.

certain extent as a gauge of the adequacy of our research efforts; that is, they can give some rough indication of the degree to which our findings come close to modeling the competency of the children we are studying.

The two examples above reflect surprisingly good memory on the part of very young children, surprising at least with reference to the developmental memory literature, where two-year-old children have seldom been asked to demonstrate memory for intervals greater than thirty seconds. There is a wide gap between the memorial competence young children show in their everyday lives and what has been studied in the laboratory. This criticism is, of course, not unique to the study of young children, but I suspect that the gap between actual level of ability and that demonstrated in psychological research is greater for very young children than for most other groups.

Narrowing this gap is a worthwhile goal for developmental psychologists. In this chapter I will argue that one way to do it is to observe young children in more naturalistic situations than has commonly been done. The assertion made here is that our estimate of basic abilities will be closely related to the extent to which our observations are conducted in settings and with tasks that are familiar and natural to the young child.

In this chapter we will be concerned with very young children's memory for locations of objects, as in the introductory examples. In the research to be described, we have attempted to develop a task that would accurately reflect the memorial competence of young children. The task has been used to investigate various aspects of early memory development, such as early evidence of self-regulatory skills (DeLoache and Brown, 1979). I will concentrate primarily on methodological aspects of the project, in keeping with the emphasis of the present volume on the usefulness of naturalistic research in memory development. Some of the research conducted so far will be described, especially studies bearing on the desirability of formulating relatively naturalistic tasks for use with very young children.

Why Study Very Young Children

This chapter considers memory in children between the ages of one-and-a-half and three years. Let us first examine some of the reasons why a developmental psychologist might want to focus on this relatively brief period. First, it is inaugurated by one of the most revolutionary changes of the life-span, the transition from sensorimotor intelligence to representational, symbolic thought. In terms of memory, the child first shows evidence of recall, rather than simply recognition (Piaget, 1968). Important theoretical issues can be raised with respect to this transition. For example, what is the nature of the representation of experience? Are there changes in its nature throughout this period? How is early memory development related to other aspects of cognitive development?

Related to the theoretical considerations that need to be addressed in research with very young children are important practical concerns. One goal in which I am particularly interested is the early detection of delayed development. Many moderately or mildly retarded children are not identified until they reach school age. It could be enormously valuable if such children could be identified earlier, during infancy or the preschool years. Early childhood (after the child has developed representational capabilities) may be an especially good time for attempting such prediction, since there is greater commonality between cognitive activities then and later in life than between infancy and later periods.

Another motivation for studying very young children is that, in spite of the important theoretical and practical issues relevant to very early development, there is relatively little research and evidence with respect to this period. We know a great deal about cognitive development in older children, and the last several years have also seen an enormous increase in our knowledge about the cognitive capabilities of infants. In between lies the uncharted territory of the toddler, where language acquisition represents the only aspect of cognitive development that has been extensively investigated.

Why Young Children Have Not Been Studied

Several factors have contributed to the relative paucity of research with very young children. One is reflected in what Brown and DeLoache (1978) referred to as the "modal memory experiment." One way to be certain of demonstrating a developmental trend is to include one group that is very young or unsophisticated relative to the memory task under study. This group can be counted on to do quite poorly and thus provide a baseline against which the progress of older, more sophisticated subjects can be evaluated. The problem with this approach, as Gelman (1978) has also noted, is that we learn relatively little about the youngest group of subjects—only what they cannot or do not do. We rarely discover much about the reasons for their incompetence in the task or what related abilities they may possess.

A second factor that has probably discouraged memory research with young children is that many of the issues that have been popular for the last several years, such as development of mnemonic strategies (Brown, 1975; Flavell, 1970) and metamemory (Flavell and Wellman, 1977) seem to have limited relevance to very young children. Wellman, however, has managed to collect some interesting data on these topics from two- and three-year-old children (Wellman, 1977; Wellman, Ritter, and Flavell, 1975). A third factor is the relative inaccessibility of this population. They are much more likely than older preschool children to be cared for at home rather than in day care centers or nursery schools and are less accessible than infants through birth announcements and diaper services.

Probably the most important factor in accounting for the remarkable absence of research with very young children is their intractability as a subject population. It is very difficult to carry out research with toddlers. Probably the two most serious difficulties concern comprehension and cooperation — getting the young children to understand what it is you want them to do and then, even more difficult, getting the children to *want* to do it. The subjects must understand the goal of the task (as defined by the experimenter) and must share that goal. It is often surprisingly difficult to meet these seemingly simple requirements, especially when it comes to subtle aspects of a task.

These research obstacles need not make us neglect this age group, but modifications in our standard research strategies may be necessary. The enormous progress in the study of infancy was made possible in large part by the development of a paradigm — the novelty preference procedure pioneered by Fantz (1963) — that could be easily adapted and applied to a wide range of memory and perceptual phenomena (see Cohen, DeLoache, and Strauss, 1979; Fantz, Fagan, and Miranda, 1975).

No such standard technique has been developed for studying young children, and it is unlikely that so simple a paradigm could take us a comparable distance. However, we would do well to emulate the infancy research to the extent of developing new procedures specifically tailored to the characteristics of our subjects. While it is perfectly legitimate and often valuable to use the same methods across species and ages, future progress will be greatly facilitated by carefully formulating tasks and procedures molded to the characteristics and inclinations of the young child rather than by trying to mold the young child into our pet paradigms. The cross-cultural research of Cole and his colleagues (Cole, Gay, Glick, and Sharp, 1971; Cole and Scribner, 1977) is instructive with respect to the danger of not giving sufficient consideration to the subject/task fit. They have amply documented the extent to which spurious inferences may be drawn about the abilities of a particular group when tested with a procedure that is inappropriate for them, even though it may be perfectly appropriate for studying the same abilities in a different group.

One way to adapt research to young children is to design research tasks to be similar to or compatible with their natural activities and situations. This is the sense in which the term "naturalistic" characterizes the research reported in this chapter.

The Continuum of Naturalism

First, what is meant here by the terms, "naturalistic" or "naturalism"? They are used in a general sense to refer to the extent to which the content, procedures, and settings of research endeavors are related to the everyday activities and environment of the subjects of the research. This usage denies the dichotomy that has too often been drawn between naturalistic and experimental approaches.

That dichotomization pits the extremes of unobtrusive observation of naturally occurring behavior in the natural environment against manipulative studies of artificial, elicited behavior in the laboratory. Two mistaken inferences frequently follow: that one approach is inherently or ultimately superior to the other; and that the two approaches do not share attributes; that is, that naturalistic settings make reasonable rigor and control impossible or that experimental manipulations are inimical to investigating "real world" activities.

Instead of seeing these approaches as divergent research strategies, we can conceive of naturalism as a continuous dimension along which research, including experimentation, can vary. (Park, 1979, has made a similar argument with respect to naturalism in research.) It is not the case that research is *either* naturalistic *or* not; rather, it is *relatively* naturalistic. In terms of the definition given earlier, research is naturalistic to the extent that it examines behaviors and processes that are (or are presumed to be) part of the subjects' everyday experience and to the extent that the research setting is or resembles the environment in which those behaviors and processes normally occur.

Thus, there are two components that are, at least conceptually, separable — the activity of interest and the environment or setting in which that activity is observed. Both of these components can be seen as falling on the continuum from artificial to natural. Therefore, both activities and settings can be relatively (more or less) natural.

The foregoing implies that we can vary the naturalism of the two components somewhat independently. For example, naturally occurring behaviors can be observed either in the child's everyday environments or in the more constrained laboratory setting. The combinations of spontaneous behavior within the natural environment and of experimental tasks in the laboratory are, of course, the familiar pure cases of naturalistic observation and standard experimentation. These "pure" approaches have proven difficult to apply to young children: classic experimentation is problematic for the reasons mentioned earlier, and naturalistic observation is plagued by problems of low base rates and uninterpretability of the behaviors of interest (see Nelson and Ross, and Wellman and Somerville, this volume).

One hybrid approach that seems to work well in the laboratory is to investigate spontaneous responses to structured stimuli or events, with a minimum of intervention by the experimenter. The less the experimenter has to instruct, lead, or cajole the subject, the better. While the setting for the research may be unfamiliar, the task is constructed so that the responses of interest are part of the child's familiar behavioral repertoire. For example, in many of Gelman's (1978) magic studies of number concepts, an important dependent variable is simply the degree of surprise shown when the number of objects in a display is surreptitiously changed.

Another strategy is to devise a game that maps into the young child's natural proclivities and interests. Most children between one-and-a-half and three years enjoy playing games such as peek-a-boo and hide-and-seek, in which objects or people (including the child) are made to disappear and reappear. In the research to be described here, a memory task was devised to resemble and be enjoyed as a hide-and-seek game. It should be stressed that the game must be one that the children do in fact enjoy and are motivated to play. It is not sufficient that the experimenter simply labels an experimental task as a "game"; the child must identify it as a desirable game to play.

Probably the most important and effective way to infuse our research tasks with naturalism is to make sure that they are meaningful to the young child (Istomina, 1975; Murphy and Brown, 1975). We probably get greater cooperation from any subjects when they understand the basic task; but older children and adults will usually comply with the experimenter's requests, even if asked to perform a meaningless, tedious activity. Young children are not nearly so responsive to others' wishes. Two-year-olds are going to do what you want them to do only if they decide that it is also what they want to do. In other words, the child must share the experimenter's goal, and young children are likely to do that only when the overall situation makes sense to them.

The other hybrid combination of task and environment involves carefully structured observations, even experiments, carried out in the child's natural environment. The approach of embedding experiments in the everyday, familiar environment has been adopted in the research to be reported here, as well as in Wellman's studies of search procedures (Wellman and Somerville, this volume; Wellman, Somerville, and Haake, 1979). An important reason for observing young children in their natural, familiar settings is to achieve ecological validity, which according to Bronfenbrenner (1977), exists when "the environment experienced by the subjects in a scientific investigation has the properties it is supposed or assumed to have by the investigator" (p. 516). Psychologists have generally assumed, or at least have behaved as though they assumed, that the laboratory or other environment has inconsequential effects on most behaviors or processes. However, we are becoming increasingly aware that this is by no means always (or perhaps even usually) true. For example, Graves and Glick (1978) have recently shown large differences between mother-infant interactions observed in the home and those observed in the lab.

An especially compelling example is provided by Acredolo (1979), who examined the effect of different environments on how nine-month-old infants searched for a hidden object. A toy was concealed in one of two cups on a table in front of the child, and then the child was moved 180 degrees to the other side of the table. Thus, the child could respond egocentrically by choosing the cup that was on the same left or right side of his body, or objectively in terms of actual spatial direction. The infants tested in unfamiliar environments (a laboratory) behaved egocentrically, while those tested in their own homes were nonegocentric. Thus, very different pictures of the infant's egocentricity emerged, depending on the environment where the testing took place. Apparently, the infants used an external frame of reference when in a familiar environment with well-known landmarks, but resorted to a body-centered frame of reference in the novel settings.

Why is it especially important to strive for greater naturalism when studying young children? Young children are "universal novices" (Brown and DeLoache, 1978); they have relatively little experience in problem-solving situations, so most experimental tasks are both new and difficult for them. Children may be forced to use a significant portion of their limited processing capability (Shatz, 1978) attending to novel features of the environment in which they find themselves or trying to figure out the details of the task with which they are confronted. Thus, fewer resources will be available for carrying out the task itself. If we limit our research with young children to highly artificial situations, we may seriously underestimate their basic competence and fail to achieve an accurate account of early development.

Furthermore, there is evidence that more complex skills, such as various forms of self-regulation (DeLoache and Brown, 1979), appear earlier for familiar, meaningful problems (Istomina, 1975). In general, emergent skills are exercised only when a person is in a relatively familiar situation and not under a great deal of pressure. Since young children must often use nascent skills to solve problems, their performance may be disrupted by even moderately unfamiliar situations. The extreme fragility of their cognitive skills is particularly characteristic of young children (Gelman, 1978).

In this regard, it is important to establish that the young child can perform adequately on some basic aspect of the task. A major problem with past research has been that when young children have performed poorly, it was not clear to what extent their performance was attributable to failure to understand or to lack of motivation to participate fully in the task. Consider, for example, a problem-solving situation, where the experimenter generally assumes that the subject is in a given initial state wanting to proceed from there to a specified final state. The researcher then studies the moves the subject makes, the strategies used, and so forth in the subject's attempt to attain the goal. However, as Klahr and Robinson (in press) have recently noted, detailed analyses of the subject's problem-solving behavior will be difficult to interpret if the subject is not actually in the assumed initial state (that it, if the child does not understand the instructions or rules pertaining to the problem) or if the subject does not share the experimenter's definition of the desired goal state (either due to failure to understand or to unwillingness to comply). There is no simple check available, such as asking the subjects what they understood about the task or what they were trying to do. Thus, if we can demonstrate that the child does well in the basic task, we can infer that comprehension and motivation are at acceptable levels. We will then have a better chance of observing more sophisticated skills in carrying it out, and perhaps be in a better position to discover what specific deficiencies underlie the child's failures.

The above recommendations are not evaluative but rather practical suggestions for more successfully enlisting the cooperation of young subjects in order to make more valid observations of their behavior. (See Gelman, 1978, for several other suggestions for recruiting young children's support.) The remainder of this chapter will be devoted to describing some current research with eighteen- to thirty-month-old children that attempts to incorporate some of these recommendations.

Young Children's Memory for Object Location

The basic problem in this research involves remembering where something is in the environment in order to retrieve it later. One of the main reasons for selecting memory for object location was to have a basic task that young children could do with some degree of competence, so that the basic task could then be used to look for more complex memory-related abilities. Performance was expected to be fairly good in this task for several reasons. The retrieval process is carried out in action—actually finding an object in the environment—rather than mentally "locating" an item stored in memory. No verbal response is required of the young child. Numerous external cues are available as memory aids, so it is not essential to generate one's own internal cues (although such cues can be produced and used). Finally, the desired goal state (including success or failure in achieving it) is obvious, even to young children.

The Hide-and-Seek Task. The memory task is presented as a game of hide-and-seek that the child plays with a small stuffed animal. The subjects initially learn the game and practice it for several days with their parents, who have been instructed by us. The children are told that Big Bird is going to hide and that they should remember where Big Bird is so they can find him later. The child watches while the parent conceals the toy in some natural location in the home (such as under a pillow, behind a door, inside a cabinet). Then a kitchen timer is set for a specified interval, and the child is told that when the bell rings he or she can go find the toy. During the interval, the children's activity is not controlled, except that they are not allowed to retrieve the toy or to remain near it. When the timer rings, the children usually jump up and immediately run after the toy. They readily learn the rules of the game and show obvious pleasure in playing it.

In the studies discussed here, the children experienced between four and eight trials of the basic hide-and-seek task on either one or two observation days. The delay intervals used were almost always either three or five minutes. (These are exceptionally long intervals for this age group. Previous memory studies with toddlers have generally employed intervals of thirty seconds.)

General Level of Performance. We have now completed five studies with a total of seventy-five subjects between eighteen and thirty months of age. The children's performance in the basic task has generally been excellent. Correct responding (going directly to the correct location with no errors of any kind) has averaged between 71 percent and 84 percent. For purposes of comparison, the subjects in the first four studies were divided into an older (twenty-five to thirty months; mean age = twenty-seven months) and a younger (eighteen to twenty-four months; mean age = twenty-one months) group. The older children generally did somewhat better; averaging over the four studies, 84 percent of their trials were errorless retrievals, while the younger group averaged 69 percent correct. Thus, it is clear that the hide-and-seek task meets the criterion of eliciting a reasonable level of memory performance from our young subjects. In fact, the older group is often very near ceiling on the basic task. This fact presents its own problems in terms of comparing the effect of different variables on the children's performance, but we find it encouraging that we have a task that better taps some of the memorial competence we believe young children possess.

Since the three- and five-minute intervals used here did not seem to give our subjects any undue difficulty, we decided to test their performance after much longer delays. To do so, we solicited the assistance of the mothers of the children in the first study. Each mother was asked to conduct five observations of her own child in the hide-and-seek game — two with thirty-minute delay intervals, two after sixty minutes, and one overnight. We warned them to be sure to place the toy so that the child could not happen upon it by chance. Since these mothers had been given extensive instructions about how to conduct the game during the pretraining phase and since we had observed them playing it with their children, we had confidence in their ability to make objective and accurate observations for us. However, as a partial check on their reports, an experimenter was present for one of the thirty- or sixty-minute observations for each subject.

The children did surprisingly well at these longer intervals. They had 80 percent errorless retrievals after the thirty-minute waits and 69 percent after an hour. They were even correct on 77 percent of the overnight trials. (Several children, after the overnight hiding, retrieved their toy before their parents got up in the morning. One poor mother told us that her child woke her at 5 A.M., wanting to go downstairs to get Big Bird.) To relieve any skepticism about the reliability of the mothers' observations, let me note that on the occasions that we formally observed, the children *always* found the toy directly. Thus, it does not seem reasonable to assume that the mothers' observations were distorted. In addition to showing the children's excellent memory, these data also attest to the extraordinary levels of motivation aroused by the hide-and-seek game.

Multiple Hiding Task. Most of the children in the first study also participated in a more complex task. On a second observation day, the same basic procedure was followed as for the standard hide-and-seek trials, except that on each trial three toys were hidden, each in a different place. After the three- or five-minute interval, the child was instructed which of the three toys to retrieve (with each serial position during hiding tested equally often). The child was then encouraged to find the other two toys as well. This multiple hiding procedure might be expected to produce a great deal of interference, since each trial involved three different toys hidden in three different locations, and sometimes a given location was used more than once over trials. Nevertheless, the children's performance was again excellent; overall, they found 70 percent of the hidden toys, with a mean of 2.1 toys retrieved per trial. These figures have been replicated quite closely in similar tasks in two other studies in this series.

It is clear from the data reported here that very young children do quite well when called upon to remember the locations of objects in the natural, familiar environment. The excellent performance in this research may be attributable to two different but related factors, each of which will be considered. One is that memory for location may be a memory skill in which children achieve proficiency relatively early. Second, specific features of the hide-and-seek game may facilitate the demonstration of that proficiency.

Development of Memory for Location

The ability to remember the locations of objects may develop early in part through demands placed upon the young child to do so. Some demands of this sort are made by the environment. To operate efficiently and successfully in the world, one has to know the permanent locations of important landmarks in the familiar environment and to remember the temporary positions of relevant objects. Huttenlocher (1974) has shown that young children first show reliable memory for the permanent locations of parts of the environment and later are able to locate objects on the basis of remembering where they were recently encountered. Among the first things that we were sure my own son knew, other than familiar people, were permanent or customary locations. For example, by seven months he would (if hungry) produce his hunger cry when carried in the vicinity of the refrigerator (without necessarily seeing it). When he was able to pull himself up to stand in his crib, he would invariably orient himself toward the door through which others would enter. Demands for remembering the location of objects also come from the child's parents. It seems likely that one of the first kinds of remembering that parents ask children to do involves location: "Where did you leave your shoes?"

Young children's memory for object locations may also be quite good because of the nature of the task itself. While it is not a recognition memory test per se, in that the subject does not simply decide whether he or she has seen something before, there are a great many external cues available to facilitate performance. The child can scan the room and be reminded of the correct location by the variety of landmarks that could be potential cues. Thus, the task might be seen as falling somewhere between pure recall and pure recognition memory tasks; the subject does have to retrieve the object, but there are many external cues available to help in the process. (Perlmutter, in press, has made a similar point with respect to delayed response tasks.)

The children's excellent level of performance in the current research may also reflect aspects of this particular task, the hide-and-seek game. As I discussed earlier, the task was specifically designed to counteract many of the problems of working with very young children. One of the primary concerns was to construct a task that would be more naturalistic than the standard laboratory tasks commonly used. For this reason, the observations were made in the children's own homes, with their parents present and participating; and the task was effectively made into a game that the children greatly enjoyed. To assess the extent to which the naturalistic features of the task were important in eliciting good performance, two experiments were conducted, directly comparing the standard hide-and-seek procedure with similar procedures judged to be of lesser naturalism.

Comparison of Tasks Differing in Naturalism

The hide-and-seek game is structurally analogous to the delayed response task introduced by Hunter (1913) to study memory in a variety of species, ranging from rats and raccoons to human children. Several recent studies have used the same procedure with children between one-and-a-half and three years of age (Blair, Perlmutter, and Myers, 1978; Daehler, Bukatko, Benson, and Myers, 1976; Horn and Myers, 1978; Loughlin and Daehler, 1973). The basic format of the delayed response task is that the subject watches while an object, usually a small toy, is hidden in one of several containers, such as boxes. After a delay interval, during which the child's attention is usually distracted away from the containers, he or she is allowed to retrieve the hidden object. Thus, both the hide-and-seek and the delayed response tasks involve remembering the location of a hidden object for a specified interval of time. The primary differences between them concern the extent to which the two tasks are naturalistic, and especially with the extent to which the memory task is embedded within a natural, familiar context.

The first study in this series directly compared the performance of two-year-old children in the delayed response and hide-and-seek tasks. All of the sixteen subjects (twenty-two to twenty-nine months; mean age = twenty-six months) participated in both tasks, in counterbalanced order. All testing was done in the children's homes. In both tasks they interacted with an experimenter who was familiar; they had previously played with her for fifteen minutes or more on at least one previous day. The hiding locations for the delayed response task were four metal boxes, each of which had a color photograph of a common object on its lid to serve as a visual cue. The children were asked to name the pictures; any labels that they failed to produce correctly were supplied by the experimenter. The naming was done in part to call the subject's attention to the pictures. The boxes were arranged in a semicircle in the middle of the floor. A different small toy was hidden in one of the boxes on each trial. After the toy was hidden, a timer was set and the subject and experimenter left that area of the room. When the bell rang, the child was encouraged to retrieve the toy. If the subject chose an incorrect box, he was allowed to search in other boxes to find the toy. The hide-and-seek procedure was exactly as described earlier. The interval for both trials was always three or five minutes.

Performance was significantly better in the hide-and-seek than in the delayed response task, with 89 percent errorless retrievals in the former and 68 percent in the latter. The figure for the delayed response task matches that reported for two-year-olds in a similar task with verbally labeled picture cues (Blair, Perlmutter, and Myer, 1978; Horn and Myers, 1978) and containers differing in size or color (Daehler and others, 1976). Of the thirteen individual subjects who had a difference in percent correct in the two tasks, eleven were superior (by 13 percent or more) in the hide-and-seek task.

These data show that in two tasks with a high degree of structural similarity, young children show significantly higher memory performance in the more naturalistic. The main differences between the two tasks in this study had to do with the hiding locations: In the hide-and-seek game, familiar natural parts of the environment were used, whereas in the delayed response task, toys were hidden in boxes with picture cues.

There are several differences between the two kinds of hiding places that might conceivably influence performance. For example, the natural locations are more separated in space. The picture cues may be less discriminable from one another than are the room fixtures. But it may be that natural locations per se facilitate performance. It may be easier to form an associative link between the toy and its location when that location is a familiar piece of furniture. Perhaps familiar landmarks are highly salient and hence effective cues (Acredolo, 1979). Or it could be that the familiar room furnishings are more readily nameable (in spite of the fact that the picture cues of fruit, toys, vehicles, and furniture used in the delayed response task were specifically chosen to be highly familiar to young children). If so, the child might be more likely to spontaneously label the hiding location at the time the toy is hidden. Further studies are planned to get at some of these issues related to the context in which the game is played. For example, hide-and-seek performance will be compared in the home versus each of two novel environments, one that is furnished in a familiar, homelike fashion (that is, with common furniture that should be easily nameable) and one that contains unfamiliar landmarks (such as laboratory equipment).

A second study also compared the standard hide-and-seek game with less natural situations. This experiment involved an amalgamation of the hide-and-seek and delayed response tasks. Each subject participated in three conditions, in counterbalanced order. One condition was the standard hide-and-seek game, with natural hiding locations used. The second condition (no landmark) was essentially a standard delayed response task, where the toy (Big Bird) was hidden in one of four plain boxes arranged in the center of the room. The third condition (landmark) involved a combination of the other two: The toy was placed in one of four boxes, but each box was located in close proximity to an identifiable piece of furniture, a potential landmark. In other words, rather than being arranged in the middle of the room, one box was on the floor next to an armchair, another was on the shelf of an end table, another on a couch, and so forth. All four boxes were always visible.

As expected, overall mean performance was highest in the standard hide-and-seek condition (75 percent), with the landmark condition second (60 percent) and the no-landmark condition last (53 percent). Thus, in general the children were most likely to find the toy when it was hidden in a natural part of the environment. However, an interaction occurred between age and type of hiding location. For the older group of subjects (mean age = twenty-six months), the standard (72 percent) and landmark (81 percent) conditions did not differ from each other, and both were significantly better than the no-landmark condition (47 percent). Thus, as long as there was some environmental feature available to mark the correct location, these children seemed to use it effectively. For the younger children (mean age = twenty-one months), the standard condition (78 percent) was significantly better than the landmark (39 percent), but the no-landmark condition (58 percent) was intermediate between the other two and did not differ significantly from either.

This pattern of results suggests a difference in the ability or tendency of the two age groups to use cues effectively. In the standard condition, where the toy is hidden in a natural location, all the children are able to associate the toy with its hiding place. How they encode and remember the correct location is not revealed by these data, but it could be done without any explicit mnemonic activity; that is, without any conscious effort to store the location. We know that information that is encountered while one is participating in a meaningful activity tends to be remembered simply as a consequence of engaging in the activity (Jenkins, 1974; Murphy and Brown, 1975). The hide-and-seek game is meaningful to the children: They understand its rules and are highly motivated to play it. Since an essential component of the game is the process of hiding the toy, it may be that all that is required for good performance is to pay attention to the hiding, to notice where the toy is being hidden. Perhaps one of the main reasons performance generally tends to be better in naturalistic tasks is that the child is usually occupied in a meaningful activity, one that involves attention to and meaningful processing of relevant information.

In addition, the familiarity of the features of the environment may facilitate encoding the correct location without intentional mnemonic effort. An association may occur more readily or spontaneously between the hidden toy and some part of the familiar, well-learned environment. If the child is already highly familiar with a given piece of furniture or part of the room, then only one additional thing needs to be learned about it — its role as a hiding place.

The landmark condition in this study would seem to require more active effort, or at least another step. Here, it is not sufficient simply to note that the toy is being hidden in a box, since there are three irrelevant boxes.

One must also code something to indicate which particular box is used: for example, the box sitting in the armchair. Thus, two steps are required—noticing and storing that the toy is hidden in a box and associating the box with a nearby landmark. The data suggest that the younger children suffer when they must form an explicit link between the hiding location (the box) and its proximal landmark.

The data for the no-landmark condition are interesting. It may be that the older and younger subjects bring different strategies to bear on this task. Since the older group is clearly sensitive to environmental landmarks and able to use them in the other two conditions, it may be that they attempt to use the same approach here. Since such cues are not available, they do poorly. The young group, who do not seem to link boxes with landmarks, may use some other basis to remember the correct box—perhaps relative position with respect to the subject's body. In other words, the two groups may attempt to use different frames of reference (Acredolo, 1979), with the older children trying to relate the boxes to the larger environment and the younger children relating them to themselves.

The results with respect to cue use are reminiscent of others in the developmental memory literature, where age differences are often found in tasks that require subjects to use mnemonic strategies, but not in tasks where such activities are not necessary (Brown, 1975). For example, in a recognition memory study using recency judgments (judging which of two stimuli appeared more recently in a series), Brown (1973) found no difference between the performance of second and fourth graders when no cues were available. However, when spatial and context cues were present, the older group effectively used them to improve their performance, but the younger subjects did not. Thus, the present results show the same developmental progression from ignoring to exploiting available contextual cues that has been demonstrated in more complex memory tasks with older subjects.

It may very well be that a familiar environment facilitates explicit use of contextual cues. In the present study, the older subjects in the landmark condition were able to associate the correct box with a nearby landmark. It is possible that they could not achieve the same result with a set of less familiar contextual cues.

Summary

If developmental psychology is ever to have a complete account of cognitive development, it will have to map the cognitive territory of the toddler. The main thrust of this chapter was to argue for more naturalistic research in addressing that task and to support the argument with data showing excellent memory performance by toddlers tested in a relatively natural situation. That research employed an experimental task that was designed to resemble and be enjoyed as a game of hide-and-seek and that was embedded in the natural environment in which such games are often played (the child's home). The results reported here showed impressive memory by toddlers for the location of objects. Comparison of performance in the hide-and-seek game with structurally similar but less naturalistic tasks revealed that the young subjects did indeed do better in the more natural situation. Several possible reasons for this were considered, including the meaningfulness of the task and the familiarity of the environment. There was also some evidence of more sophisticated use of contextual cues by the older subjects (two-year-olds) in one of the conditions.

References

Acredolo, L. P. "Laboratory Versus Home: The Effect of Environment on the Nine-Month-Old Infant's Choice of Spatial Reference System." *Developmental Psychology,* 1979, *15,* 666–667.

Blair, R., Perlmutter, M., and Myers, N. A. "The Effects of Unlabeled and Labeled Picture Cues on Very Young Children's Memory for Location." *Bulletin of the Psychonomics Society,* 1978, *11,* 46–48.

Bronfenbrenner, U. "Toward an Experimental Ecology of Human Development." *American Psychologist,* 1977, *32,* 513–531.

Brown, A. L. "Mnemonic Elaboration and Recency Judgments in Children." *Cognitive Psychology,* 1973, *5,* 233–248.

Brown, A. L. "The Development of Memory: Knowing, Knowing About Knowing, and Knowing How to Know." In H. W. Reese (Ed.), *Advances in Child Development and Behavior.* Vol. 10. New York: Academic Press, 1975.

Brown, A. L., and DeLoache, J. S. "Skills, Plans, and Self-Regulation." In R. Siegler (Ed.), *Children's Thinking: What Develops.* Hillsdale, N.J.: Erlbaum, 1978.

Cohen, L. B., DeLoache, J. S., and Strauss, M. S. "Infant Visual Perception." In J. Osofsky (Ed.), *Handbook of Infancy.* New York: Wiley, 1979.

Cole, M., Gay, J., Glick, J., and Sharp, D. *The Cultural Context of Learning and Thinking.* New York: Basic Books, 1971.

Cole, M., and Scribner, S. "Cross-Cultural Studies of Memory and Cognition." In R. V. Kail and J. W. Hagen (Eds.), *Perspectives on the Development of Memory and Cognition.* Hillsdale, N.J.: Erlbaum, 1977.

Daehler, M., Bukatko, D., Benson, K., and Myers, N. "The Effects of Size and Color Cues on the Delayed Response of Very Young Children." *Bulletin of the Psychonomics Society,* 1976, *7,* 65–68.

DeLoache, J. S., and Brown, A. L. "Looking for Big Bird: Studies of Memory in Very Young Children." *The Quarterly Newsletter of the Laboratory of Comparative Human Cognition,* 1979, *1,* 53–57.

Fantz, R. L. "Pattern Vision in Newborn Infants." *Science,* 1963, *140,* 296–297.

Fantz, R. L., Fagan, J., and Miranda, S. "Early Visual Selectivity." In L. Cohen and P. Salapatek (Eds.), *Infant Perception: From Sensation to Cognition: Basic Visual Processes.* Vol. 1. New York: Academic Press, 1975.

Flavell, J. H. "Developmental Studies of Mediated Memory." In H. W. Reese and L. P. Lipsett (Eds.), *Advances in Child Development and Behavior.* Vol. 5. New York: Academic Press, 1970.

Flavell, J. H., and Wellman, H. M. "Metamemory." In R. V. Kail, Jr., and J. W. Hagan (Eds.), *Perspectives on the Development of Memory and Cognition.* Hillsdale, N.J.: Erlbaum, 1977.

Gelman, R. "Cognitive Development." *Annual Review of Psychology,* 1978, *29,* 297–332.

Graves, Z. R., and Glick, J. "The Effect of Context on Mother-Child Interaction: A Progress Report." *The Quarterly Newsletter of the Institute for Comparative Human Development*, 1978, *2*, 41–46.

Horn, H. A., and Myers, N. A. "Memory for Location and Picture Cues at Ages Two and Three." *Child Development*, 1978, *49*, 845–856.

Hunter, W. S. "The Delayed Reaction in Animals and Children." *Behavior Monographs*, 1913, *2*, 1–86.

Huttenlocher, J. "The Origins of Language Comprehension." In R. L. Solso (Ed.), *Theories in Cognitive Psychology: The Loyola Symposium*. Washington, D.C.: Winston, 1974.

Istomina, Z. M. "The Development of Voluntary Memory in Preschool-Age Children." *Soviet Psychology*, 1975, *13*, 5–64.

Jenkins, J. J. "Remember That Old Theory of Memory? Well Forget It." *American Psychologist*, 1974, *29*, 785–795.

Klahr, D., and Robinson, M. "Formal Assessment of Problem-Solving and Planning Processes in Preschool Children." *Cognitive Psychology*, in press.

Loughlin, K. A., and Daehler, M. A. "The Effects of Distraction and Added Perceptual Cues on the Delayed Reaction of Very Young Children." *Child Development*, 1973, *44*, 384–388.

Murphy, M. D., and Brown, A. L. "Incidental Learning in Preschool Children as a Function of Level of Cognitive Analysis." *Journal of Experimental Child Psychology*, 1975, *19*, 509–523.

Park, R. D. "Interactional Designs." In R. B. Cairns (Ed.), *The Analysis of Social Interactions*. Hillsdale, N.J.: Erlbaum, 1979.

Perlmutter, M. "Development of Memory in the Preschool Years." In R. Green, D. Linkenhoker, and L. McCarron (Eds.), *Childhood Development*. Lexington, Mass.: Lexington Books, in press.

Piaget, J. *On the Development of Memory and Identity*. Barre, Mass.: Clark University Press, 1968.

Sugarman, S. *Scheme, Order, and Outcome: The Development of Classification in Children's Early Block Play*. Unpublished doctoral dissertation, University of California, Berkeley, 1979.

Shatz, M. "The Relationship Between Cognitive Processes and the Development of Communication Skills." In B. Keasey (Ed.), *Nebraska Symposium on Motivation*. Lincoln: University of Nebraska Press, 1978.

Wellman, H. M. "Preschoolers' Understanding of Memory-Relevant Variables." *Child Development*, 1977, *48*, 1720–1723.

Wellman, H. M., Ritter, R., and Flavell, J. H. "Deliberate Memory Behavior in the Delayed Reactions of Very Young Children." *Developmental Psychology*, 1975, *11*, 780–787.

Wellman, H. M., Somerville, S. C., and Haake, R. J. "Development of Search Procedures in Real-Life Spatial Environments." *Developmental Psychology*, 1979, *15*, 530–542.

Judy S. DeLoache is an associate professor in the Department of Human Development and Family Ecology at the University of Illinois. She received her Ph.D. degree in Developmental Psychology in 1973 from that institution, and was subsequently a research associate at the Center for the Study of Reading and Cognition there.

*A summary of memory-related quasi-naturalistic research is
presented and the important features and requirements of
using such an approach with toddlers is discussed.*

Quasi-Naturalistic Tasks in the Study of Cognition: The Memory-Related Skills of Toddlers

Henry M. Wellman
Susan C. Somerville

A fundamental goal of cognitive developmental research is "to get inside the head" of the child at different ages. This is a difficult goal to achieve, encompassing many obstacles to valid interpretation and engendering frequent discussion about research methods. Because this is an elusive goal, once a task or paradigm is found which successfully reveals internal processes it is used often and adapted to many purposes: witness the use of the Sternberg task, the Brown-Peterson paradigm, sentence verification tasks, serial recall and semantic organization paradigms by adult and developmental psychologists alike. Unfortunately use of this research armament is problematic for getting inside the head of the preschooler, especially the one-, two-, or three-year-old toddler. These paradigms require verbal sophistication, speeded responses,

Preparation of this chapter was supported by NIH grant 1 R01HD13317–01 to
the authors.

ability to deliberately focus attention and effort, willingness to cooperate with strangers, and application of cognitive processes to novel tasks or tasks removed from the context of everyday experiences. All of these features pose obstacles for revealing the cognitions of preschoolers and toddlers. These features are partly responsible for the negative description of the preschooler which pervades the literature: current descriptions depict what preschoolers can *not* do (Gelman, 1978). The same features account for the paucity of information on toddlers' cognitive functioning; two-year-olds often will not minimally comply with the demands of such procedures.

If one approaches the assessment of toddler's cognition from the opposite direction similar obstacles arise. The infant habituation paradigm has been remarkably useful in revealing the hidden cognitive capacities of infants. However, the habituation paradigm requires its own forms of subject compliance and predictability and it is applicable to only a narrow range of responses. This makes it of limited usefulness with toddlers who possess different and increased response capabilities. Thus, an important lacuna exists in our knowledge: What developments bridge the gap from the remarkable but primitive cognitive capacities of the infant to the already considerable skills of the five-year-old?

The one area where investigations within this gap are relatively detailed is language development. Part of the reason for this seems to be that in language acquisition research it has been possible to record and analyze the child's naturally occurring utterances. This approach places few atypical demands on the young child, yet has provided a sizable, revealing data base. Can this method, observing the child's naturally occurring behavior, profitably be used to study other domains of cognitive development in the toddler? In particular, can it be used to describe the development of early memory processes? The research presented in this chapter began with this question. Thus, the orientation of the work has been away from the classic paradigms of cognitive psychology. It rests instead on analyzing the everyday cognitive tasks and accomplishments of toddlers. However, after a few initial attempts we have avoided a purely observational, nonmanipulative research strategy. Why *not* just collect young children's natural outputs, as is often done in psycholinguistic research? The reasons are that unlike language many important memory behaviors occur only infrequently (see Spiker, 1977), occur in noisy, confounded, hard-to-interpret forms, and are difficult to observe directly since they are internal representations and processes. For example, at an early point in our considerations we recruited parents of young children for a naturalistic diary study. They were to record behaviors of their child that were related to memory and memory-like processes. These diaries were replete with examples where children were instructed to remember something (for example, to remember to feed the cat). However, by observation alone it was impossible to tell how accomplished children were on these everyday memory tasks (because the caretakers would remind the child to feed the cat or do it themselves with little or no opportunity being given for the child to remember or fail to remember).

Our current research strategy entails the use of what could be called quasi-naturalistic tasks. These are tasks that are either embedded in or inspired by the natural accomplishments of children and the situations of childhood. However, the tasks and situations have been converted to our experimental purposes by the generation of controls or comparisons which eliminate alternate interpretations. Thus, in all our studies we have standardized and regularized noisy everyday events and responses in order to collect interpretable data. In what follows we present a summary of our memory-related quasi-naturalistic research to date. Then, drawing on this research for examples, we consider some of the important features and requirements of using such an approach with toddlers. We conclude with a discussion of the usefulness of drawing a distinction between naturalistic and laboratory or experimental methods.

The Research

The early diaries, mentioned above, were quite useful in one respect. These records indicated two general classes of memory situations faced repeatedly by younger children: memory for future activities and memory for the location of objects. Examples of the first class include remembering to brush your teeth before going to bed, remembering to say grace before meals, reminding mother to buy milk at the store, reminding father to buckle his seatbelt on entering the car. Examples of the second class include remembering where you put your coat, remembering where the forks go, searching for misplaced keys by remembering where you saw them last. These two categories of naturally occurring tasks have provided the inspiration for more controlled quasi-naturalistic studies reviewed below. It is important to preface this review by noting that in this research we have not attempted to isolate "pure" memory processes. Instead, the research examines a family of tasks, all of which are memory related. The tasks require the encoding and recall of remembered information in order to retrieve knowledge, actions, or objects. This research will be summarized in two overlapping sets: first, the research on memory for future activities and second, the research on search strategies, which are based on memory for the location of objects.

Memory for Future Activities. Even young children often brush their teeth at the appropriate time, feed the cat daily, and say prayers at night. Is this because they are constantly prompted to do so, or do they recall such routines on their own? In a study of children's memory for routines (Somerville, Wellman, and Cultice, 1980), we addressed this question using a revised, standardized diary format that provided important controls.

One-, two-, and three-year-olds were studied in this research. In consultation with the child's caretaker one routine task per child was chosen for study, such as saying grace or feeding the fish. Each caretaker received careful instructions for observing and recording behavior, all incorporated into a scripted diary. The primary purpose of this script was to allow sufficient time for the children to remember on their own. Thus, each day at the appropriate time for the routine to occur the child was to be given a minimum of five minutes to remember to engage in the appropriate routine spontaneously. Only after this did the caretaker provide, first, a visual prompt (folding hands for grace), then a verbal prompt ("what do we do before we eat?"), and finally, if needed, instruction to the child ("don't forget to say grace").

Half the children were observed for six days on an established routine, which was already a regular part of the families' daily activities. For the other half, caretakers began a new daily routine for the child. Performance on old routines was high and stable across days for all children. Even one-year-olds remembered old routines about 75 percent of the time with only a visual prompt. Performance on new routines was, as expected, poor on the first days. However, two- and three-year-olds (but not one-year-olds) became significantly more accurate at remembering new routines over the course of just six days. Indeed three-year-olds' performances on old and new routines were essentially at ceiling after six days. Thus two- and three-year-olds were able to recall new routines after only a few days practice. Careful scrutiny of the routines showed that they were roughly consistent across ages; it was not the case that older children's recall tasks were just easier.

This standardized diary study had certain advantages, namely the collection of infrequently occurring but informative data by the person in the best position to record it. There were also disadvantages. Most importantly, it was not possible to verify the mothers' observational reliability, since having a second observer influenced mother and child and was not feasible in some of the routines under observation. It was therefore conceivable that mothers just expected older children to be better, and so credited them with more success. To provide convergent validation of the results on household routines we undertook to study children's memory for routines in their nursery school classroom, using blind, trained, reliable observers (Somerville, Wellman, and Cultice, 1980). A preschool class of two-year-olds and a separate class of four-year-olds who met on different days in the same classroom were observed. The two routines of interest were the same for both classes, and revolved around snack time. One was washing hands after classroom cleanup and before being seated for snack. The second was throwing away the empty juice cup after snack and before going to the reading corner for a group story.

Once again, in order to collect interpretable data, teachers cooperated with us by standardizing their behavior and instructions. Most importantly, they refrained from instructing children to wash up or to throw their cup away, until an appropriate late place in the sequence of events. Thus children all had some time for spontaneous remembering. We collected data both on children's compliance with the routines, and the sequence of naturally occurring prompts they received. In the handwashing case all children received a standardized "five-minute" warning, telling them that cleanup was imminent, followed by a "now" instruction telling them it was now time to put things away. In addition to these nonspecific verbal prompts, a child might receive other nonspecific verbal prompts, visual prompts (another child washes hands), specific other prompts (another child is told to wash hands), and finally a specific target prompt might be given (target child told to wash hands). Similar prompts could occur for the cup routine.

Twelve children were observed at least four times each on both tasks in the spring of the year. The final rates of compliance were equal for the two- and four-year-olds. That is, almost all children performed appropriately at some point, indicating that all could comply and that none were just resistant to the routines in general. However, few two-year-olds remembered spontaneously (for example, after only the first nonspecific prompt, remembering occurred on only 6 percent and 15 percent of instances of washing hands and discarding the cup respectively). Four-year-olds often remembered with this minimal level of cueing (31 percent and 40 percent for the same two tasks). In general it required more prompts and more specific prompts to induce the two-year-olds to remember as often as four-year-olds.

Given the differences in method, the results of the observational study were consistent with the earlier diary study in indicating age differences in memory for routines based on the amount and type of prompting received. Both studies also indicated a relatively high level of recall by young children given helpful but nonspecific prompts. With this validation we returned to the standardized diary procedure for a study of reminding. In our original work caretakers said that they would, sometimes facetiously, ask their child to remind them to do things (such as hanging up the wash), and would often be surprised when their one- or two-year-old later carried out their request. Remindings of this type are intriguing. Unlike routines which can be learned over the course of numerous similar trials, this sort of reminding is often a unique occurrence and, if reliably performed by the child upon instruction, represents a more obviously deliberate memory-related behavior. If the child recalls the activity subsequently simply because he or she was instructed to do so earlier, this constitutes reasonable evidence of adopting a deliberate set to remember (see Wellman, 1977a). In addition, since caretakers could easily devise different types of reminding tasks, this provided an opportunity to test factors which might determine the child's performance. We conducted a reminding study (Somerville, Wellman, and Cultice, 1980) with two-, three-, and four-year-olds. The essence of the task was that the caretakers asked the children to remind them to do something. On different days caretakers chose reminding tasks that differed both in interest level and in length of delay. Tasks were of high or low interest to the child (such as buying candy at the store versus hanging up the wash), and required a short delay (one to five minutes) or a long delay (from morning until afternoon, or night until morning) before reminding. Each child received two different high interest-short delay tasks, two high interest-long delay, two low interest-short delay, and two low interest-long delay tasks over the course of eight days. Recording and prompting procedures were almost identical to those in the first routines study. For each reminding task the child was given at least five minutes to remember spontaneously followed by a visual prompt, a verbal prompt, and then instruction.

The largest effect was the difference in performance between high versus low interest tasks. High interest tasks resulted in spontaneous reminding about 70 percent of the time whereas low interest tasks were much harder, resulting in only about 20 percent recall. In contrast, length of delay, while a significant factor, had much less effect (45 percent versus 35 percent spontaneous success for short and long delays). Significantly, there were no effects of age in this analysis; all children performed equally well or equally poorly depending on the interest level of the task. We believe the absence of age differences resulted from task selection. Having caretakers pick tasks of specific significance to their child meant that the selected tasks were adapted to the child's understanding and interests.

In sum, these data extend those from the earlier two studies. In all studies even the youngest children performed at relatively high levels in some conditions (old routines, high interest remindings). The developmental differences obtained seemed due to differences with age in the amount of time required to establish appropriate cues to recall—as for example in how long it took to establish new routines—and the number and strength of cues necessary at recall to provide memory (visual cues versus spontaneous recall). The results of the interest level manipulation were especially relevant to explaining these cued recall effects. Careful analysis of tasks chosen for the high and low interest conditions revealed that tasks chosen to be of high interest were likely to be part of a social action sequence that was thoroughly understood by the child (for example, eating food, or a child-oriented event such as going to the zoo). Low interest tasks were likely to be less understood (for example conveying information to a third party, or initiating an adult oriented task such as putting clothes in the dryer). Thus children's prevailing knowledge of the structure and significance of events and routines (Chi, 1978; Nelson, 1978) would be likely to provide certain necessary and useful *internal* cues to future events. In this case, four-year-olds, more than two-year-olds, may be able to remember to throw their cups away after snack because they comprehend more of the reasons why this is necessary and know more about the typical mealtime script that makes cues such as the *end* of snack more naturally salient or available. At the same time, both children may be able to remind mother of a future task, if the task is suited to their respective levels of understanding and desired goals.

The picture of toddlers' memory abilities painted by this research seems more optimistic than Perlmutter and Myers' (1979) conclusion garnered from more laboratory-like tasks: "None of the children performed very well . . . there seemed to be a paucity of effective processing and no evidence of deliberate strategy use" (p. 81). In contrast, our data clearly indicate effective processing. As this quotation indicates, the question of the early development of deliberate memory processing is also an important one. The reminding research suggests that young subjects can adopt a deliberate "set to remember" if instructed. But what of deliberate strategy use? What sort of deliberate activities, if any, can young children bring to bear to ensure later memory? More detailed information about this question was collected by Wellman, Ritter, and Flavell (1975).

In this research, two- and three-year-olds were presented a task where a toy dog was hidden in a series of locations. After each hiding, the experimenter left the room, instructing half the children to "wait with the dog" and half to "remember where the dog is." Each child's behavior during the delay was recorded through a one-way mirror. The performances of three-year-olds were clear. Three-year-olds looked at the hiding place during the delay more when instructed to remember than when instructed to wait, and some engaged in other obvious strategies such as retrieval practice (for example, looking at the target location and nodding *yes*, looking at other locations and nodding *no*) and making the target location distinctive (for example, resting their hands on it throughout the delay; moving that container to a salient position). Importantly, children instructed to remember recalled more than those instructed to wait, and those engaging in higher levels of strategic behavior indeed were more accurate in their recall.

The data from two-year-olds was uninterpretable. Two-year-olds were anxious about being left alone in the room, wanted their mothers present which subsequently distracted them, and often found the hidden item immediately, neither "waiting" nor "remembering."

In short, these hidden dog studies indicated the presence of certain simple, external memory strategies in young three-year-olds. There was no evidence of classic mnemonic strategies such as verbal rehearsal or encoding, clustering, or elaboration. Yet certain behaviors such as looking and touching were deliberately mobilized to aid in the solution of an obvious everyday problem, remembering where a toy is. Two-year-olds may or may not employ similar or other devices.

Search Strategies. The hidden dog studies can be conceived of as an investigation of memory for future acts and also as an investigation of children's search. The type of search behavior required here involves procedures for finding remembered but missing objects in an extended environment (that is, extended, behavioral search as opposed to purely visual search or perceptual detection). Extended behavioral search is an observable and memory-related activity of young children, including toddlers. These children go to their toy boxes to search for certain toys, go to special hooks or closets or drawers to find their clothes, they know where forks and cups and milk are usually kept and so where to first search for them. Somewhat older preschoolers are often amazingly proficient at such games as concentration; they enjoy and spontaneously initiate hide-and-seek and Easter egg hunts.

In the hidden dog studies the specific concern was young children's utilization of deliberately employed procedures to prepare for *future* retrieval. Similarly, subjects can engage in efforts at *current* retrieval of remembered information or objects. The investigation of search for remembered missing objects can thus be seen as a natural extension of the previous studies: focusing on strategies for coping with current retrieval demands, as opposed to strategies for preparation for future retrieval. In our initial research on this topic (Wellman, Somerville, and Haake, 1979), two- through six-year-old children searched for a lost object on their nursery school playground. Eight locations were marked on the playground in a roughly semicircular arrangement by utilizing in-place playground equipment (for example, slides, sandbox, jungle gym). Each child had two searches. In the first, the free search, the locations were pointed out and the child was asked to search for a missing item. After this search, the child was taken to each location sequentially and at each location did a short task (tire hopping, sandbox jump, and so on). On this tour, the child's picture was taken at location 3. Subsequently, at location 7, another picture was to be taken but the camera was missing. The tasks at locations 7 and 8 were quickly completed and then the child searched for the camera. This second search was termed the logical search. If the subject recalls that location 3 was the last place the camera had been seen and that location 7 was the first place it was discovered missing, then the logical search strategy would be to search only in locations 3 through 6, the critical search area.

At all ages, children were more likely to first search in the critical area in logical search than in free search. They also directed a significantly larger proportion of their first four logical searches to the critical area (70 percent) in comparison to their first four free searches (50 percent). In free search they tended to search all locations end to end. In logical search they were more likely to exclude noncritical locations from their search altogether and to repeatedly search the critical area.

A second study involving search through a series of eight indoor cupboards found similar results. Both of these search studies nicely demonstrated the use of deliberate retrieval strategies on the part of even the youngest children. The children's modification of their search pattern between free search and logical search and the appropriateness of behavior in the logical search condition evidenced employment of the critical information to direct search for a remembered object.

In addition to deliberate modification of retrieval behavior there was also evidence of apparent logical skill on the part of young children; they limited search to the logically critical area. This was surprising. Further consideration of the playground data suggested the following. The most common first search in the logical condition was at location 3, where the picture had been taken. However, location 3 could have been first searched because it was the location with the highest association with the camera ("that's where we took my picture") or because of its role in defining the critical area ("that's the last place we had the camera"). Analysis of the second searches of those children who first searched at 3 was consistent with the notion that younger children searched in a spatial-associative fashion (based on the spatial association of the camera with location 3), whereas older children more clearly understood the critical area. For example, second searches of young children were less likely to remain in the critical area than those of older children. Both types of retrieval strategies rely on remembered information about past locations of the object, but they differ in how such information is used to direct search.

The conclusion that younger children used remembered information in a spatial-associative manner could only be tentatively accepted from these results; the appropriate subsequent analyses could be conducted with less than half the subjects. In fact, the conclusion that older children were using logical retrieval strategies was also shaky. Because of the special associations of location 3 even apparently logical search could have been initiated by or enhanced by salient association. For these reasons we conducted another playground study (Haake, Somerville, and Wellman, in press). At a different school and different playground, preschoolers, three-and-a-half-years-old and up, were tested. As in the first playground study, subjects performed free and logical searches of eight locations. Logical search conditions establishing a lost camera were conducted in two different fashions: a picture-at-3 condition identical to the original study and a contrasting picture-at-1,2,3 condition. In picture-at-1,2,3 the camera was used to take the child's picture at all the first three locations. Search directed to the critical area in this picture-at-1,2,3 condition must depend on location 3's importance as the last place the camera was seen, not just an association with where a picture was taken. In this condition, a spatial associative search strategy should lead one to locations 1, 2, and 3, not the critical area.

The results were clear. In both conditions children at all ages significantly directed search to the critical area (more than was true in free search and more than expected by chance). Spatial associative search to just locations 1, 2, and 3 was conspicuous by its absence. Thus for children aged three-and-a-half and older deliberate, logical search strategies were confirmed.

Because it is typically difficult to get nursery schools which can permit researchers to monopolize their playground, and because for the school used in this second playground study the population was aged three-and-a-half and up, this study could not investigate younger children. However, in a study by Sophian and Wellman (1980) we have researched even younger children's ability to utilize remembered information to logically guide search.

To introduce this study, consider the following problem. Suppose you have to find the scissors and you remember that they are usually kept in a kitchen drawer, but also remember that yesterday you were using them to cut string in the basement. How should the two pieces of remembered information be combined to determine where to search? In this instance, you could logically ignore the first information and go to the basement. On the other hand, suppose you need to find the scissors and your spouse tells you they are in the back of some drawer, and you remember the specific kitchen drawer where they are usually kept. In this case you could combine both pieces of information to best limit search. These examples reveal two important points. First, search often requires the integration of general remembered information (you usually keep it there, scissors are in the kitchen drawer) and more immediate context-specific information (I just used it in the basement, my spouse says it's in the back of the drawer). Second, integrating this information has a particular assymetrical logic to it. Sometimes remembered information should be combined to reduce search, sometimes the same information should be ignored.

The Sophian and Wellman study examined logical searches of this type with young preschoolers (aged two and three), old preschoolers (aged four and five) and first graders (aged six and seven). Children searched for small toys in a replica apartment house. The upstairs of the building had one apartment of two rooms — a bedroom and a kitchen. The downstairs was identical. Each child conducted searches when there were varying types of general information present — some search objects were specifically associated with one room (pillow: bedroom, cereal: kitchen) and some were equally associated with either room. The searches also varied in the amount of context-specific information present — sometimes the child was told what type of room it was in (in a kitchen, in a bedroom, upstairs, downstairs). In this situation children could just rely on the general associations to guide search. Or they could combine information where appropriate (for example, if told to search upstairs for cornflakes, would they go to the upstairs kitchen) and avoid the same information if it was inappropriate (for example, if told to search for cornflakes in the bedroom, would they avoid the kitchen). This task nicely revealed young children's abilities. Most importantly, there were few age differences. Even the youngest children combined the two pieces of information when appropriate. They also avoided inappropriate searches in the situation where the two pieces of information conflicted (more than would be expected given their knowledge of the items and to the same extent as the oldest children). Thus they did not just search on the basis of general spatial associations: they used such information selectively to appropriately limit retrieval efforts.

In sum, very young preschoolers combined relevant remembered information to search logically. Indeed, this has now become a familiar pattern. In continuing our investigations, Robert Haake has devised a simplified version of the critical search task, which involves hiding an object under one of six upside down buckets, and showing the child either that the object is still in the experimenter's hand at some point or that the hand is now empty. Preliminary results show that even the two-year-olds limit their first search to the critical area. Their consistency in doing so is far from perfect, but they modify their behavior significantly as compared to free searches.

Summary. The studies described have yielded a number of important conclusions. Evidence bearing on two classic ontogenetic topics, early capacity for recall or active retrieval and processes contributing to that capacity and its development, concerning memory has been generated.

Current theories postulate that recall capacities develop in late infancy or soon after in the toddler. Thus investigations of toddlers' recall capacities are especially important. Studies of routines and of remindings demonstrated early and relatively impressive recall capacities in one-and-a-half- and two-year-olds. This included reliable cued recall over delays of up to a day. The hidden object studies demonstrated young children's ability to recall the location of objects and thereby successfully retrieve them.

Of course, demonstrations of such capacity in toddlers is only a start. What factors determine accurate performance and what processes contribute to the development of recall? The present research indicates three such factors. First, there is the development of a deliberate set to remember, an ability to recall information at a later time because of an earlier instruction (from self or other) to do so. The presence of such an ability in such young children (two-year-olds) is an important finding of the reminding research. The ability to set oneself the goal to remember is prerequisite to all later development of intentional strategic (planful, efficient) memory.

Second, there is the development of deliberate mnemonic strategies to ensure accurate retrieval. At least in external memory tasks, tasks requiring memory for the location of objects in the external environment, young children were shown to be developing a repertoire of strategic processes. Evidence has been generated of storage strategies such as making hiding places distinctive (Wellman, Ritter, and Flavell, 1975), maintenance strategies such as maintaining a visual fixation on the location over the course of a delay (Wellman, Ritter, and Flavell, 1975), and retrieval strategies such as the logical utilization of remembered information to pinpoint an object's location (Sophian and Wellman, 1980; Wellman, Somerville, and Haake, 1979). In this research there has been no demonstration of the three classic memory strategies of rehearsal, clustering, and elaboration. Such verbal and imagery-dependent strategies may indeed be outside the scope of the young child's knowledgeable utilization. On the other hand, other logical and effective memory-related strategies were employed by very young children to ensure remembering and to ensure accurate retrieval.

Third, there is the development of knowledge structures. Increasing understanding of the sequence and significance of events accounts for accurate recall in a variety of everyday memory tasks. Extending other work (Chi, 1978; Nelson, 1978), present research on routines and reminding suggests the role of increasing knowledge structures in partly explaining developing memory abilities. Knowledge differences also are likely to be found in memory-related search (such as searching in a familiar as opposed to unfamiliar search space).

The present research does not, as yet, provide the basis for a comprehensive theory of memory development in the toddler. However, it has uncovered a number of promising techniques for revealing early memory abilities and has provided substantial information about the early development of memory processes.

Methodological Implications

In addition to substantive findings, the research reviewed has touched upon numerous issues of experimental methodology in the study of young children's cognition. The study of very young children is fraught with a number of specific obstacles to interpreting their behavior, many of which were encountered in the present research. These obstacles can be translated into a set of methodological requirements, which deserve explicit discussion. In general, the tasks used to investigate the cognition of the very young child should be engaging to the child, thoroughly understood by the child, tailored to the child's goals and response capabilities, yet rigorously interpretable. For all of these reasons the use of quasi-naturalistic tasks, controlled extrapolations from the everyday tasks of childhood, seems a productive research strategy. Four specific concerns and requirements are detailed below.

1. One requirement is the demonstration of positive results, findings describing what the toddler can do. The reason for seeking positive results is that often, with very young children, positive results are relatively interpretable but equivalent negative results are not. Consider the Wellman, Ritter, and Flavell (1975) deliberate memory studies. Finding that three-year-olds deliberately modified their behavior in certain memory-related ways in the remember condition, as compared to the wait condition, constituted fairly reliable proof of attained memory skills. However, finding that two-year-olds did not do so did not necessarily mean that the same skills were absent. The young child's fear of strangers, misunderstanding of the instructions, and the like, could all be masking legitimate mnemonic abilities. With young children there are always such conceivable or demonstrable factors which make findings of incompetence suspect. Thus a first step is to find valid instances of the competency and abilities which are present. Careful scrutiny of apparent naturally occurring abilities is often an important first step here.

Once one has a context of positive abilities within which to describe the child, then valid negative information is also required. Descriptions of the child's capabilities should be linked with statements about limitations; the factors of task difficulty and cognitive load which combine with ability to yield less than perfect performance on many occasions. However, given what was said above, special care is needed to yield valid negative results. One clear research strategy is to contrast positive and negative results in a single study. For example, once it had been demonstrated that young children were accurate at recalling high interest, short delay tasks then their failure to be accurate on low interest short delay tasks became informative. Both tasks were presented with the same instructions and under the same conditions. Positive performance in one situation could thus usefully be compared to negative performance in the second. In short, positive demonstrations of ability on some task must be compared with valid negative findings to generate informative developmental descriptions and theories. Ingenious combinations of different conditions and careful selection of contrasting but comparable tasks within the same investigation are required (see also Siegler, 1978).

2. In the deliberate memory studies (Wellman, Ritter, and Flavell, 1975), performance in the remember condition was compared to performance in the baseline wait condition; in the deliberate search studies (Wellman, Somerville, and Haake, 1979; Haake, Somerville, and Wellman, in press), logical searches were compared to free searches. It is often essential to assess the baseline response choices of children in a given task situation. Such assessment serves two functions. First, the young child's skills normally are sufficiently inconsistent and influenced by changing patterns of attention and intention, so as to be demonstrable only with appropriate comparisons. For example, in the Wellman, Somerville, and Haake (1979) study, young children averaged only 2.7 of their first four searches in the critical area in the logical search conditions. Without knowing that this pattern was significantly different from free searches it would not have been possible to decide that this was a logical modification of their behavior (even though a modest one). Thus, baseline comparisons allow detection of false negatives. The second function served is the detection of false positives. Notice, in the logical search task, that children could search first and most often in the critical area for nonlogical reasons. In particular, the logical area was in the middle of the array and thus directly in front of them. Also in linear arrays (as in Wellman, Somerville, and Haake, 1979, study 2; Drozdal and Flavell, 1975) the middle of the array would be closest to the start point. Only the comparison of logical with free searches enables one to rule out the possibility of apparently logical searches stemming from other response tendencies. The general point is that young children's behavior is multiply determined. Thus, it is important to know the a priori probabilities of their exhibiting the responses of interest. This controls potential behavioral biases for and against certain responses which are used to index cognition.

3. One of the most important requirements of working with young children is communicating the task to them. Perhaps the largest source of erroneous interpretation of young children's behavior stems from observing children on tasks where the experimenter instructs or expects them to do one thing but where they actually do something else (Donaldson, 1978). Two strategies can be used to combat this problem: tasks can be chosen that stand a good chance of being understood by the child, and relevant data can be collected in order to confirm that the task has been understood. As to the first strategy, the key function served by modeling tasks and situations on the everyday tasks of

childhood is to generate tasks likely to be understood and accepted by the child. Such quasi-naturalistic tasks are comprehensible and familiar and can also be fun and engaging. A refinement of this strategy is to choose comparable general tasks for all subjects (such as household routines) but to test each subject on a specific version (such as remembering to feed the cat) that is particularly familiar and understood by that child.

Even with the most "natural" of tasks, however, it cannot be assumed that the task will be understood; comprehension of task instructions and conditions must be empirically demonstrated. One possible demonstration is eliciting positive results; if the child succeeds at the task, he or she must have understood a good bit about it. A second approach is the use of warm-up or pretest tasks. Warm-up and pretest tasks that are simple analogs of the later focal task are presented to the child to test that the child understands crucial aspects of the instructions and procedures. At the same time, these examples can be used to teach the child what is desired (see Wellman, 1977b). Finally, a detailed analysis of the child's responses can often show that certain plausible misinterpretations of the task have not occurred (see Wellman, Ritter, and Flavell, 1975).

The strategies, or some combination of them, can be used to overcome the fact that young children's understanding or approach to the task situation is often demonstrably different from that of an adult, and often different from the investigators' desires. Thus a variety of manipulation checks are needed to assess the nature of the task for the child.

4. The final consideration in this section is perhaps the most important. No one situation or task and no one measure of ability is definitive of children's skills. Every demonstration is imperfect; it has its demonstrable or potential flaws. This is nowhere more clear than in working with inconsistent, hard to instruct, wary young children. Thus, by necessity, investigators must provide a converging web of evidence. The more numerous and independent the ways in which certain strengths and weaknesses of the child are demonstrated, the less likely it will be that some important source of invalidity (misunderstanding of instructions, inattention, boring tasks, inconsistent abilities) has influenced the results. The specific inadequacies of any one study or measure, and these are always present no matter how naturalistic yet controlled the task is, can be partly overcome in a different study.

The Distinction Between Naturalistic and Experimental Approaches

Throughout this chapter there has been a tendency to contrast naturalistic and controlled experimental methods. Indeed, discussions concerning the study of cognition and its development often draw a pervasive contrast between experimental and naturalistic research methods. When discussed by its advocates, experimental research is reputed to be precisely focused, statistically and conceptually powerful, and demonstrably free of a litany of sources of invalidity. When discussed by its detractors, it is narrow, statistically significant but often practically trivial, and when concerned with developmental and cross-cultural competencies, laden with false negatives. In contrast, naturalistic research, when discussed by its proponents, is reputed to be ecologically valid, representative of the full range of human cognitive skills, sensitive in detecting the child's significant cognitive achievements, free of sources of external invalidity (such as lack of generalization), and the ideal vehicle for testing the social and practical relevance of laboratory findings. When evaluated by its critics, naturalistic research is held to be productive of largely descriptive and obvious generalizations, inefficient or insensitive for collecting data on infrequently occurring events or unobservable states and processes, seriously confounded by naturally occurring covariates, and best considered as exploratory or pilot research.

As may be obvious from the above paragraph, these two approaches need not and probably can not be validly contrasted. Use of naturalistic or laboratory-experimental tasks does not ensure reaping the rewards described earlier, nor does it inoculate the research against the complementary disadvantages. In fact, the key issue is not the use of experimental *versus* naturalistic methods, but the ingenious construction and exploitation of suitable methods to yield converging and valid results. In the specific case of research with very young children, exploiting the child's naturally occurring behavior and goals has certain special advantages, and failure to at least take these into account has clear liabilities as detailed above. Thus, with the toddler we believe quasi-naturalistic tasks have a special role to play. Such tasks represent controlled extensions or manipulated simulations of naturally occurring tasks and situations. Ingenious use of such tasks allows the investigator to avoid numerous sources of invalidity.

The present research is not the only example of quasi-naturalistic approaches. Returning to the introduction of this chapter, recent language acquisition research with very young children, in acknowledging the limitations of merely analyzing spontaneous productions, has turned to similar devices. In such studies, investigators have used "semi-naturalistic settings" (Bridges, 1979), in-the-home situations designed for individual children (for example, Thompson and Chapman, 1977), and the comparison of spontaneous productions with elicited samples (for example, Anglin, 1978). To reiterate, however, the promise of this research has little to do with its being termed quasi-naturalistic. The use of tasks inspired by or embedded within naturally occurring events offers a productive research strategy, but the strength of such a strategy is founded on specific, valid, and generalizable findings, not on assertions of naturalism per se.

References

Anglin, J. M. "From Reference to Meaning." *Child Development,* 1978, *49,* 969–976.
Bridges, A. "Directing Two-year-olds' Attention: Some Clues to Understanding." *Journal of Child Language,* 1979, *6,* 211–226.

Chi, M. I. H. "Knowledge Structures and Memory Development." In R. S. Siegler (Ed.), *Children's Thinking: What Develops?* Hillsdale, N.J.: Erlbaum, 1978.

Donaldson, M. *Children's Minds.* New York: Norton, 1978.

Drozdal, J. G., and Flavell, J. H. "A Developmental Study of Logical Search Behavior." *Child Development,* 1975, *46,* 389–393.

Gelman, R. "Cognitive Development." *Annual Review of Psychology,* 1978, *29,* 297–332.

Haake, R. J., Somerville, S. C., and Wellman, H. M. "Logical Ability of Young Children in Searching a Large-Scale Environment." *Child Development,* in press.

Nelson, K. "How Children Represent Knowledge of Their World in and out of Language: A Preliminary Report." In R. S. Siegler (Ed.), *Children's Thinking: What Develops?* Hillsdale, N.J.: Erlbaum, 1978.

Perlmutter, M., and Myers, N. A. "Development of Recall in Two- to Four-Year-Old Children." *Developmental Psychology,* 1979, *15,* 73–83.

Siegler, R. S. "The Origins of Scientific Reasoning." In R. S. Siegler (Ed.), *Children's Thinking: What Develops?* Hillsdale, N.J.: Erlbaum, 1978.

Somerville, S. C., Wellman, H. M., and Cultice, J. "The Development of Memory in Toddlers: Memory for Routines and Reminding." Unpublished manuscript, University of Michigan, 1980.

Sophian, C., and Wellman, H. M. "Selective Information Use in the Development of Search Behavior." *Developmental Psychology,* 1980, *16,* 323–336.

Spiker, D. "An Observational Study of Problem-Solving Behavior in Six Preschoolers." Paper presented at meeting of the Society for Research in Child Development, New Orleans, 1977.

Thompson, J. R., and Chapman, R. S. "Who Is 'Daddy' Revisited: The Status of Two-Year-Olds' Overextended Words in Use and Comprehension." *Journal of Child Language,* 1977, *4,* 359–375.

Wellman, H. M. "The Early Development of Intentional Memory Behavior." *Human Development,* 1977a, *22,* 86–101.

Wellman, H. M. "Preschoolers' Understanding of Memory-Relevant Variables." *Child Development,* 1977b, *48,* 1720–1723.

Wellman, H. M., Ritter, K., and Flavell, J. H. "Deliberate Memory Behavior in the Delayed Reactions of Very Young Children." *Developmental Psychology,* 1975, *11,* 780–787.

Wellman, H. M., Somerville, S. C., and Haake, R. J. "Development of Search Procedures in Real-Life Spatial Environments." *Developmental Psychology,* 1979, *15,* 530–542.

Henry M. Wellman is an assistant professor of psychology at the University of Michigan. He received a Ph.D. degree from the University of Minnesota's Institute of Child Development, and previously served on the psychology faculty at Arizona State University.

Susan C. Somerville is an assistant professor of psychology at Arizona State University.

Methodological and theoretical concerns motivating more ecologically valid procedures for exploring children's remembering are discussed and findings from a study combining observational and experimental techniques are presented.

The Role of Social Context in Memory Development

Hilary Horn Ratner

The study of memory development has largely revolved around understanding the child's ability to plan, execute, and monitor strategies to encode and retrieve information in laboratory situations (see Brown, 1975; Flavell, 1970; Flavell and Wellman, 1977; Hagen, Jongeward, and Kail, 1975 for reviews). Although research has broadened in recent years to include study of representation (for example, Kosslyn, 1978), constructive processes (for example, Paris, 1978), and the influence of the knowledge base on memory (for example, Chi, 1978; Perlmutter and Myers, 1976) among others, a significant aspect of memory functioning still has been generally overlooked. Little attention has been focused on the child's ability to remember in naturally occurring situations, which, especially for the young child, comprise most of the remembering children do and undoubtedly influence remembering in more structured settings. Approaches involving more ecologically valid procedures, including observation, need to be implemented to begin to explore children's remembering in a variety of contexts. Methodological and theoretical concerns provide motivation for pursuing such an approach and these concerns

This research was supported by a grant from NICHHD (No. HD90346) awarded to Nancy Angrist Myers and Marvin W. Daehler and was written while the author was supported by NIMH National Research Service Award 1 F32 MHO7743-01.

will be explored here. Findings from a study combining observational and experimental techniques will be presented and the utility of the approach evaluated.

Orientation of Past Research

Although children's memory has long been studied (for example, Hunter, 1913, 1917), memory development has been an area of intense research concern only in the last fifteen years. The recent rise in attention primarily resulted from the growing interest in cognitive processes that occurred within experimental psychology in general. The information processing model of memory (see, for example, Atkinson and Shiffrin, 1968) became predominant in cognitive psychology and its widespread acceptance led to its application developmentally as well.

Memory in this model is depicted as compartmentalized into sensory, short-term, and long-term stores, with control processes responsible for maintaining information within memory and transfering information among the storage components. Variations in the nature and use of the control processes, or strategies, were found to influence how much could be remembered. Researchers became interested in whether children's remembering was controlled by similar processes. Tasks used in studying adults, such as remembering lists of words under various conditions, which primarily involve short-term memory abilities, were modified for children (see, for example, Brown and Scott, 1971; Flavell, 1970; Goldberg, Perlmutter, and Myers, 1974; Perlmutter and Myers, 1979; Rossi and Wittrock, 1971), who were found to remember less and to use strategies less often and effectively than adults, although these abilities increased with age. Because strategy use was found to affect the amount of information remembered by adults and children's growing ability to remember paralleled their increasing ability to use strategies effectively, the changes in strategy have been seen, at least in part, as accounting for age differences in amount of information remembered. In addition, or as an alternative, changes in the capacity of the three storage components have been viewed as contributing to the increasing ability of the child to remember. Thus a model to interpret developmental changes, a set of issues to study, and a method for studying them have been borrowed directly from investigations of adult remembering.

Limitations of Research on Memory

This progression in the study of children's memory development has had several effects on the field. First, almost no descriptive work has been conducted on the child's memory development. Experimental psychology in general has evolved without the preliminary descriptive stage that natural sciences have passed through (Hutt and Hutt, 1970) and has been criticized for losing touch with the natural phenomenon studied (Neisser, 1976). When the information processing model was applied to children's memory, this bias toward manipulative experimental control without adequate knowledge of the potentially modifiable behavior was further entrenched in developmental investigations of memory. Furthermore, because little consideration was given to the effect on memory functioning of the individual's goals, the need to determine the child's memory behavior in contexts other than the laboratory was not perceived.

Adoption of the information processing model and consequent use of list learning tasks have limited understanding of preschool children's memory development to a greater degree than that of the school-aged child. Standard tasks are difficult to conduct with very young children and as a result relatively fewer investigations of the preschooler's memory abilities have been conducted. Although investigators have begun to develop other types of tasks more amenable to the behavioral repertoire of the preschooler (Daehler and O'Connor, 1980; Horn and Myers, 1978), knowledge of the preschool child's memory abilities is still scant. The two-to-four-year-old child often performs fairly poorly in the laboratory, especially on recall tasks (Myers and Perlmutter, 1978) and has been described as a nonstrategic, nonplanful, and nonactive rememberer. Because the preschool child's memory performance has not been observed in a wide variety of settings, however, it is difficult to evaluate the significance of his poor performance. The context of the laboratory may be rather limiting and not allow a full display of the young child's capabilities.

Theoretical Importance of Observations

Support for pursuing an observational approach has been motivated largely by methodological concerns or at least by the unavailability of observational information. There are, however, more theoretically based reasons for undertaking this approach.

Soviet View of Memory Development. The use of observational methods becomes more critical, for example, in exploring Vygotsky's sociohistorical model of cognitive development, modified and extended by researchers in the Soviet Union. Several reviews of the Soviet work are available (Cole and Scribner, 1977; Smirnov and Zinchenko, 1969; Yendovitskaya, 1971) and only a brief description relevant to our purposes will be provided here.

Soviet psychologists have long viewed cognition in general and memory in particular as developing within the context of social interactions which in turn are dependent upon larger historical and cultural forces. Marx, whose writings formed the basis for Vygotsky's thinking, proposed that man's mental life should be approached as the product of community life and that consciousness from the beginning of time has been an historical product (Leontiev and Luria, 1968). Vygotsky recognized the importance of these ideas and believed that psychological functioning must be understood in terms of its origin and development and that social interactions underlie this development (Wertsch, 1978).

Children's remembering is thought to be initially controlled by the structure of the external environment and not by activities solely engaged in for the purpose of remembering (Yendovitskaya, 1971). That is, children do little to help themselves remember and the young child's remembering occurs as a by-product of play, daily events, and comprehension. With increasing age the child's remembering becomes defined as a goal within itself and comes under conscious control, first by relying on external means of remembering and then on more advanced internal means. All higher psychological functions, including memory, are thought first to occur between people, such as mother and child, before being internalized by the child alone (Vygotsky, 1978). For example, the child may initially remember events only when questioned in certain ways by the mother or when interacting with her in certain contexts. Eventually the child may come to use these very means, questioning and contextual retrieval cues, to promote remembering on his own. Presumably, as the child grows older, parents increase their demands and further facilitate the growth of memory abilities. The demands made on the child to remember and recall, which are originally shared by mother and child, aid the child in developing the means to voluntarily remember. Acquisition of memory skills, then, is thought to be rooted in the social activities of daily life and parents are seen, at least in part, as instrumental in bringing about the shift from involuntary to voluntary memory. It is important to note that although Vygotsky stressed the importance of cultural influences on cognition, he viewed development as a complex interweaving of both biological aspects of behavior and socio-historical demands of an individual's culture.

According to the Soviet view of memory development, then, the child's social interactions are central to the development of memory skills. Because children in our society, especially very young children, spend much of their time interacting with their mothers, mothers would provide much of the input involved in facilitating memory growth. In order to understand the development of memory, then, we should be interested primarily in the content and structure of interactions between mothers and children, which promote its development. Observations of mothers and children interacting with one another in the context of their daily activities should provide important information about memory development. Surprisingly, not even Soviet psychologists have conducted these observations. An observational approach could be used, then, to investigate what sorts of memory demands children encounter in social interactions and whether these demands play an important role in the development of memory.

Cross-Cultural Cognition. Recent cross-cultural investigations, in addition to the Soviet perspective just described, have suggested that daily experiences are central to the shaping of cognitive functioning (Kagan and others, 1979; Sharp, Cole, and Lave, 1979; Stevenson and others, 1978; Wagner, 1974, 1978; Wilkinson, Parker, and Stevenson, 1979). Memory performance of schooled and unschooled populations was compared in these studies. Children attending school generally remembered more or used memory strategies more effectively. Kagan and others (p. 60) found as well that education of the family head correlated with memory performance and these authors speculated "that some families may be implementing practices or communicating values to their children that facilitate memory performance." Obviously it is not the family into which one is born or what school is attended that accounts for these differences found in memory functioning. As these authors suggest, it is the interactive experiences of the child, with parents or teachers, within all of these social contexts, in conjunction with the biological makeup of the individual, which influence the development of memory. However, the cognitive experiences provided in school or within the family that account for differences in memory between schooled and unschooled populations are as yet unknown. Neither is it understood which experiences in everyday life give rise to the cognitive competence found among unschooled children. To acquire this information, observations of these daily situations must be made so that the experiences which influence cognitive development and account for differences among individuals will be understood.

Description of Study

Rationale. Observations of children at home, at school, and at play in various cultures and subcultures appear to be crucial to our understanding of how daily experiences influence cognition and development. Such observations are needed to extend and corroborate previous findings, to generate new hypotheses and tasks, to evaluate memory performance in different settings, and to test theoretical memory models which emphasize social interactions in cognitive development. As a beginning attempt to answer some of these questions, a combination of observational and experimental procedures was used to examine the nature of memory demands placed on young children by their mothers and the role these demands may play in the child's memory development. Differences in demands as a function of the child's age, how the demands were met, and the relationship between memory demands and memory performance were studied.

Subjects. Five boys and five girls at each of two ages, thirty and forty-two months, and their mothers participated in the study. Potential subjects were located from birth records and their mothers were sent a letter describing the project. Mothers were then telephoned and visits were scheduled if mothers were interested in participating.

Mothers and children were white, middle to upper middle class residents of Amherst, Massachusetts and surrounding towns. Mothers averaged 2.2 years of education past high school with a range of 0 to 8 years. Only three mothers were working outside the home at the time the observations were conducted, and these worked only part-time or an evening shift. All of the children were home reared and only two of the older children attended nursery school part of the day. Three of the children were only children, eleven had one sibling, five had two siblings, and one had three. Of the children with siblings four were first-born.

Procedure. Trained observers visited the children's homes for four two-hour sessions over a two-week period. Conversations between mothers and children as they went about their daily routines were tape-recorded and written down by the observer with accompanying notes on ongoing activities. Transcriptions were made of these conversations and utterances involving memory demands were coded. After the observations were completed, children participated in a laboratory task designed to tap long-term memory.

Dependent Measures. Memory demands may take many different forms, such as requiring the retrieval of information, storage of information, giving of instructions, and providing of memory-specific information or general knowledge of how memory works. Prior to the actual study, informal observations of mothers and children were carried out to provide preliminary information as to what types of demands children were encountering and which ones should be studied. On the basis of these observations, memory demands investigated in this study were limited to demanding retrieval of information and providing memory-specific information.

Memory Demands. Answering questions that occur in conversation requires the retrieval of information; because asking questions occurs fairly frequently in mothers' speech (Cross, 1977; Holzman, 1972; Newport, Gleitman, and Gleitman, 1977) this type of demand was thought a good one for study. Even children at the very beginning stages of language acquisition appear to discriminate questions from statements and to discriminate *wh*-questions from *yes-no* questions (Crosby, 1976; Ervin-Tripp, 1970; Horgan, 1978). Since children provide different types of responses to each type of utterance, children appear to know they are being asked to retrieve information and to make a response.

Various question forms also require different degrees of memory processing and represent varying levels of demands. For example, a *wh*-question asks who, what, when, where, why, or how and requires the retrieval of a specific piece of information as an answer. A *yes-no* or *verification* question asks only for the verification of a proposition and requires a response of either *yes* or *no*. In the first case, recall is required and in the second, recognition. While it is not always the case that recognition is a less difficult task than recall (Tulving and Thomson, 1973; Watkins and Tulving, 1975), in general it has been found that information is more easily recognized than recalled (Kintsch, 1970; Klatsky, 1975) and this is true for children as well as adults (Myers and Perlmutter, 1978). To investigate whether memory demands as well as their memory performance increase with the children's age, we can ask if the incidence of recall and recognition demands increases with the child's age and if the child is more successful in answering *yes-no* questions than *wh*-questions.

Mothers' questions also differ in what is asked. Types of information requested for retrieval may vary with the child's age and children may be more successful in responding to certain types of questions depending on content. For example, mothers have been found to predominantly center their conversations on the here-and-now (Cross, 1977; Ervin-Tripp, 1978; Snow and others, 1976) by limiting their discussions to what the child can see and hear, what is about to happen, and what has just happened. How often children are asked about past events when their conversations are centered primarily on the present may be very important in memory development. Incidence of asking and relative ease of answering questions may also depend on whether the question deals with various types of object information. For example, providing the name of an object or remembering its characteristics or location may be less difficult than recalling events.

Memory-Specific Information. The extent to which mothers provide information about memory functioning represents another way the child may learn about memory from daily social interactions. Retrieving information may provide the child with useful but indirect memory experiences. Being provided information about memory directly, however, may be much more essential in developing memory skills. In fact, knowledge of memory, or metamemory, has been viewed by some as very central to the development of memory abilities (Flavell, 1979; Flavell and Wellman, 1977). Flavell and Wellman speculate that the child may acquire metamemory, at least in part, as a result of interactions with parents either directly or indirectly through conversation and activities. Thus, any information given the child or skills effectively modeled for him may be an important source of memory knowledge.

Cross-Situational Memory Behavior. A final area of focus was the child's memory performance within different settings and the relationship between performance and mothers' memory demands. The child's memory performance was measured by examining responses given to the mother's questions, by counting the frequency of spontaneously remembered events not produced as responses to questions, and by performance on two long-term memory tasks, a production and verification task. In these tasks the child was shown a large empty dollhouse and two rooms were pointed out and named as the kitchen and bathroom. In the production task, children named all things they could that would be found in one of the rooms. After all items possible were named, the verification task was begun in which twenty-four miniature replicas of objects, half appropriate and half inappropriate room items, were given children who were asked if each belonged in the room. For example, appropriate kitchen items included stove, refrigerator, coffee pot, and frying pan. Inappropriate items included piano, razor, sandbox, bed, and couch. This procedure was repeated for the other room.

The production and verification tasks were chosen because information well known to the child, previous to his coming to the laboratory, was involved and a wide range of responses possible. The questions in the production task also seemed to resemble those asked by mothers at home. This allowed the comparison of the child's ability to retrieve information from long-term memory in response to questions asked at home and in a structured task. Furthermore, because the production and verification tasks and mothers' questions involved retrieval of information from long-term memory, a relationship between demands and performance might be more likely found; and if found, the basis for the relationship more apparent.

Question Coding. Particular sentence types were identified and coded from the transcriptions of the home conversations. Each question was coded for both form and content. Form referred to whether a *wh-* or *verification (v)* question was asked. Only utterances of an interrogative form which appeared to actually seek information were coded, however. Many questions such as "Why don't you open the window?" or "Can you close the door?" are actually indirect, polite ways of instructing someone to perform an act, not ways of asking for information (Ervin-Tripp, 1976). Some utterances taking a question form which were aimed at producing an action on the part of the child were of interest, however. For example, "Can you count for me?" is a request for the production or recall of information, that is, an ordered series of numbers, and therefore was coded as a *wh-*question.

Content referred to what was talked about in the question and was divided into two broad categories, event and knowledge, which were further subdivided to characterize the exchange more precisely. Event questions in general referred to activities or mental experiences of people in certain time contexts. The subdivisions made in this category primarily reflected when the events occurred. Presumably it would be more difficult to retrieve information about events occurring some time in the remote past as opposed to those occurring at the present time and the demand placed on memory functioning greater in the first than second case. The questions coded in the knowledge category were in some ways more diverse than event questions. These questions dealt with generalized, semantic information about objects for the most part, although some questions were concerned with contextual, episodic knowledge as well. The more frequently occurring content subdivisions, with examples, are listed in Table 1.

Findings

Event and Knowledge Questions. Mothers questioned their children frequently; about one-fourth of their total speech was involved in questioning at each of the two ages and approximately two-thirds of these questions dealt with events. The proportion of mothers' questions dealing with events increased with age, although the actual number nonsignificantly decreased, (61.5 percent at age two; 69.6 percent at age three) and knowledge questions decreased with age both proportionally and in frequency. The proportional increase in event questions, however, was largely due to an increase in asking only one

Table 1. A Partial List of Event and Knowledge Subdivisions (Examples of Selected Categories Appear in Parentheses.)

EVENT

1. *Ongo* — ongoing events.
2. *Past Immediate* — events occurring no more than fifteen minutes before question is asked.
3. *Future Immediate* — event occurring no more than fifteen minutes after question is asked.
4. *Future* — events occurring at least fifteen minutes in the future.
5. *Within Session* — events at least fifteen minutes before question is asked, but during the current observational session.
6. *Total Session* — events during the period in which observations are first begun and ended, but not on the current day of observation.
7. *Before Session* — events before sessions ever began.
8. *Other Remote Past* — events some time in the past and not on day of observation, but exact time is unknown.
9. *Habitual* — events occurring repeatedly and representing past, present, and future state of affairs.

KNOWLEDGE

1. *Object and Animal Names*
2. *Person Names*
3. *Object Locations* — ("Where is your bike?")
4. *Object Properties and States* — ("What color is an apple?").
5. *Social Routine* — information about what people are expected to say or do in certain social situations ("What do you say to the lady?").
6. *Object Comparison* — comparison of two objects on one dimension or in general ("What do you have that's like this toy?").
7. *Object Pretending* — information concerning objects used in play sequences ("What's that?" — referring to a block of wood the child is moving back and forth).
8. *Personalized Object Knowledge* — objects or people known to the child from a personalized episodic context ("What kind of shoes do you want from the store?").
9. *Symbol* — information about letters, numbers, or words.
10. *Visual or Auditory Materials* — repetition of or information about songs, stories, television, etc. ("How does that song go that Donny sings on the record?").
11. *Objects Experienced in Past Contexts* — ("Was Uncle John driving a yellow car yesterday?").

type of question: the repetition or clarification of what the child had just said. Question form did depend on the information requested. At both ages a larger proportion of questions was asked in the *wh*- than verification form (26.2 versus 12.3 percent at age two; 20.1 versus 10.3 percent at age 3). For event questions, two-year-olds were asked more verification than *wh*-questions (37.0 versus 24.5 percent), while at age three there was not a significant difference between mothers' asking of *wh*- and *v*-questions (31.1 versus 38.5 percent). The proportion of *v*-questions, then, did not change with age, whereas *wh*-

questions increased and *wh*-knowledge questions declined with age. Clearly, then, mothers did not ask more questions or demand more recall from older than younger children as might be expected.

At both ages about half of the event questions asked dealt with events that had just taken place, were currently happening, or which were to occur momentarily. Some mothers, however, were found to consistently broaden the context of their questions to past and future events, removed from the past in time or space. Remote past questions accounted for 14 percent and future event questions 5 percent of all the event questions. Questions dealt with events occurring one hour to one year before the question was asked. Even young children, then, were expected to remember information from the quite distant past and to recall it in response to these specific questions. Mothers who questioned their children frequently about past events asked relatively fewer questions about present events. Even though all mothers tended to talk primarily about present events with their children, some mothers were consistently more likely than others to introduce discussions of the past into their dialogues.

Mothers who asked many event questions were likely to also ask many questions concerning knowledge of objects, symbols, and routines ($r = .76$, $p < .01$ at age two; $r = .53$, $p < .05$ at age three). Among mothers, a wide variety of knowledge questions was asked but individual mothers were consistent in asking similar types of questions. Names, locations, and properties of objects and people were most frequently asked about and mothers who asked many of one type asked many of the others. Other less frequently asked questions, which involved information about objects experienced in particular contexts, were also consistently asked by some mothers.

Correct Responding to Questions. In general, questions were not answered correctly very frequently at either age — only about one-third to one-half of the questions asked. When children did not answer questions correctly, they usually failed to respond rather than answering incorrectly. At both ages verification questions in the knowledge category were more frequently answered than *wh*-questions (56.9 versus 36.7 percent at age two; 56.0 versus 45.6 percent at age three); however, only the two-year-olds answered more verification than *wh*-event questions correctly (52.0 versus 39.2 percent at age two; 56.3 versus 58.0 percent at age three). The ability to answer correctly *wh*-questions in the event category increased between ages two and three and three-year-olds were as successful in answering the *wh*- as *v*-event questions. Although children improved in their ability to answer questions, then, they were not able to easily retrieve information when specifically requested to do so, or were not motivated for some other reason to answer these questions.

Question Demands. Mothers did not uniformly require more memory processing of older than younger children by demanding more recall than recognition, by consistently demanding the retrieval of more difficult information, or by demanding the retrieval of information more often. Age-related increases in memory ability found in this study and in other research cannot be attributed to increasing memory demands with increasing age. The cross-sectional design of this study, however, may have interfered with observing these changes and therefore a longitudinal design may be more sensitive in assessing developmental increases in memory demands. For example, some mothers talked to their children very little and others a great deal, but this was not generally consistent with the child's age. It is possible that, although level of questioning differs considerably among mothers, most increase their questions across time. Individual differences, then, may have obscured observing this possible increase and thus observations of the same mothers should be conducted over time. On the other hand, it may be that memory demands do not increase between ages two and three, at least in the form of questions, or are not primarily responsible for the age-related memory changes which occur. Perhaps memory demands vary across children but stay relatively stable between these ages and account better for differences among children at one age. Perhaps as long as adequate environmental stimulation is provided, the development of memory abilities proceeds; however, environmental stimulation above a base level may lead to higher levels of memory functioning at one particular age.

Memory-Specific Information. Although mothers frequently asked questions, they provided little knowledge about memory directly to their children. The number of sentences involved in exchanges concerning memory was counted; however, such occurrences were rare and no differences between ages were observed. Examples of instruction on the part of the mothers to aid recall included one mother's description of a mnemonic device to remember an actor's name and another mother's instruction to put the child's boots by the door so he would be sure to wear them when he went outside. Thus, occasionally mothers did provide information on how to best use memory abilities. Children even less often demonstrated any knowledge or sensitivity to memory processes. Nevertheless, one two-year-old boy, upon the unexpected return of his father after leaving home for work, asked "What Daddy forgot?" and a two-year-old girl asked her mother to call the family dog into the house so she could draw a picture of him because she had forgotten what he looked like. These examples, though rare, were still an impressive indication of even two-year-olds' knowledge of memory-related situations. Learning about memory clearly begins at a very early age; however, the two-year-old child is not a very sophisticated rememberer even within a highly meaningful social context.

Another potential source of information about remembering was the use of the word *remember*. *Remember* occurred fairly infrequently in mothers' speech and not more often by mothers of older than younger children (12.8 times at age two and 9.2 times at age three). However, older children themselves used *remember* more frequently than younger children (1.8 versus 0.3 times) and mothers' use of *remember* correlated with the child's use of the word ($r = .82$, $p < .01$). *Remember* appeared significantly more often in a question as,

"Do you remember x?" than in a statement or more importantly than in an instruction as, "Remember to do x." Mothers did not typically instruct their children to specifically remember something for a future time. Children, then, heard the word in its retrieval sense far more often than in its encoding sense. This is interesting considering that when young children are told to remember a set of items, they perform no differently than if told simply to look at the items (Appel and others, 1972). Young children may primarily know the word *remember* in its retrieval sense from their mothers' use of the word and not realize they are being told to perform some special behavior. Alternatively, young children may have problems planning ahead in memory tasks and mothers may be sensitive to these difficulties thereby using *remember* more often in its retrieval than encoding sense.

Relationships Between Memory and Memory Demands. At both ages children performed very well on the verification task, although performance did increase significantly with age from 89.6 percent to 97.9 percent correct. When correct responses to appropriate and inappropriate room items were examined separately, however, two-year-olds were as successful as three-year-olds in identifying the appropriate room items (94.2 percent for two-year-olds and 96.3 percent for three-year-olds). The younger children's difficulty came in successfully rejecting inappropriate items (85.0 versus 99.6 percent). Although the knowledge of two- and three-year-olds matched, the younger children had extreme difficulty retrieving what they knew in the production task. Only an average of 2.2 items for both rooms was produced at age two, while at age three, 7.9 items were given.

A major focus of the study was whether the types of questions asked by mothers at home and the frequencies in asking them would be related to performance on the verification and production tasks conducted in the laboratory. At age two neither the rate with which questions were asked nor the types of questions asked were significantly correlated with either verification or production performance, except for a negative correlation between *wh*-event questions and production. Two-year-olds, however, performed uniformly poorly on the production task and were generally uncooperative even in the verification task. Task performance did not vary greatly among the children and as a result, relationships between mothers' questions and children's performance was undoubtedly difficult to detect. In order to suitably test the relationship between memory demands and memory performance in the future, a memory task must be found in which two-year-olds are willing to participate and in which a larger range of responses is obtained. Although methodological difficulties cannot be ruled out, it may be that memory demands and performance are simply not related at age two. Children at this age may have difficulties even comprehending many of the questions asked them (Ervin-Tripp, 1970, 1978) and therefore may not be attempting to retrieve the information requested. They may know that they are being asked to retrieve and respond, but not what specific information to retrieve. Therefore, questions may not be serving a memory function and would not be expected to be correlated with memory performance.

For three-year-olds, several relationships were found between mothers' questions and children's memory performance. When the event and knowledge question categories were considered as a whole, performance on the verification task was positively correlated with the frequency of asking both event ($r = .65$, $p < .05$) and knowledge questions ($r = .60$, $p < .05$), while production performance was related only to asking event questions ($r = .60$, $p < .05$). Thus, children whose mothers made more memory demands in the form of asking particular types of questions performed better on the memory tasks.

When the relationships between asking event and knowledge questions and memory performance were examined in more detail for the three-year-olds, the asking of particular types of questions emerged as primarily responsible for the correlations. In general, questions dealing with present events were not correlated significantly with production and verification performance or were significantly negatively correlated. Questions dealing with the past (that is, total session, before session, and other remote past) were significantly positively correlated with performance on one or both of the memory tasks. Children whose mothers asked many questions about past events which required retrieval of information about events removed from the present were best able to retrieve information from long-term memory. Children whose mothers asked many questions about present events which required memory retrieval, but not for information about events removed from the immediate context, were least able to retrieve information from long-term memory. Therefore, the asking of questions in general is not the important factor in the relationship between memory demands and memory performance; it is the asking of questions concerning past events which require retrieval of information not recently experienced. Quite specific memory demands, then, appear to be responsible for the relationship between memory demands and performance.

Fewer significant correlations between question types and memory performance were obtained when correlations were computed for the knowledge question subtypes. Significant correlations that were obtained occurred more often between knowledge question types and verification than production performance. The significant correlations that did emerge in relation to production occurred between memory performance and those questions concerning objects in changing contexts, such as object-pretend and objects experienced in past contexts. This evidence, as well as the stronger relationship between production and event questions than knowledge questions, suggests that the retrieval of information which is contextually unique may involve an important type of memory demand. Children may need to make use of creative retrieval skills to comprehend and answer questions concerned with contextually bound information. Knowledge questions, which decreased with age, may have been part of well-practiced routines and may have required fairly passive execution of search routines. If memory demands do influence memory performance, the retrieval of well-practiced information needed to comprehend and answer questions may be useful to some extent in developing further abilities required in production tasks.

The relationships between memory performance, mothers' and children's use of the word *remember* and other demonstrations of metamemory were tested as well. For three-year-olds, verification performance correlated with the number of times *remember* was used in a question by both mother ($r = .67$, $p < .05$) and child ($r = .62$, $p < .05$), as did production performance with mothers' ($r = .62$, $p < .05$) and children's ($r = .68$, $p < .05$) use of *remember*. At age two, these measures were negatively correlated with memory performance. Direct demonstration or instruction concerned with memory functioning was not correlated with memory performance at either age. Therefore, children may have been learning something about what it means to remember indirectly through their mothers' use of the word, but not through direct instruction. Flavell and Wellman's (1977) suggestion that significant others provide aliments and demands that shape the child's own thoughts rather than serving as models of memory behavior appears more likely correct.

Although the correlations between memory demands and memory performance establish that the two are related, at least for the older children, it is not at all clear that mothers' memory demands actually shaped children's memory functioning. For example, just the reverse may have occurred; children's memory abilities may have influenced mothers' demands. The child who produces many items on the production task may remember well at home and may prompt his mother to ask him many questions. Since mothers' questions concerning past events were correlated with production performance, these questions were recoded as initiated spontaneously by the mother or elicited by the child. The proportion of child-elicited questions was then correlated with production performance. If the child leads the mother in questioning him, then a positive correlation should be found between the two measures. Instead, the two were negatively correlated and the correlation was marginally significant ($r = -.52$, $p < .10$). If anything, then, children who often elicited maternal questions about past events tended to perform more poorly on the production task. This evidence still does not rule out the possibility that children were in some way influencing the frequency and type of their mothers' questions; however, this result does support the opposite conclusion. Of course, there is still the possibility that some underlying factor influenced both mothers' demands and children's performance and accounted for the correlations found.

Cross-Situational Memory Performance. To have some idea of how consistently children were remembering in the laboratory and at home, performance on the production task was correlated with both the proportion of *wh*-questions answered correctly (knowledge and event categories separately) and the number of spontaneously remembered events, past events recalled by the child that were not responses to questions or cued by mothers. All three measured the child's ability to recall information from long-term memory under different conditions and might be expected to be positively correlated if retrieval in all three instances were governed by similar mechanisms. Production was not significantly related to the child's ability to answer his mother's questions at either age two or three; however, the relationship between production performance and spontaneously remembering events is somewhat stronger, at least for the older children ($r = .45$, $p < .07$). This is the only evidence, then, that retrieval from long-term memory is relatively consistent in two quite different settings. It is interesting that performance consistency is apparent only for the three-year-olds, suggesting that as the child grows older he becomes more able to use a common set of skills for retrieving information rather than being solely influenced by the context in which remembering takes place. This interpretation is strengthened somewhat by the finding that again only at age three is there a positive correlation between production and verification performance ($r = .43$, $p < .10$).

Utility of the Observational Approach

At the beginning of this chapter, I claimed that an observational view of children's memory was needed to balance the laboratory-experimental work that has dominated the study of children's memory development. Because virtually no description of children's memory behavior outside of the laboratory was available, we did not have evidence supporting conclusions made about the young child's development from several contexts, we did not have descriptions of memory functioning in everyday life, and we have not used tasks or studied issues that have been derived independently from studies of adult memory functioning. We knew little about the consistency of performance in different settings and whether meaningful social interactions would support very young children's memory functioning to a greater degree than that observed in the laboratory.

From the variety of questions asked children by mothers it was obvious that children are exposed to a vast array of information that they are expected to remember and that is not usually tapped in laboratory settings. For example, children were asked to remember locations of objects both permanently and temporarily placed, object property information, personalized information about objects, social routines, habitual events, past events, future events, and more. Indeed, a diverse set of categories had to be created in order to adequately describe the content information involved in mothers' questions. Even though mothers' questions represent only one type of memory demand, these descriptions begin at least to catalogue memory demands the child faces every day. I have been unable to report here the types of memory demands encountered through instructions given children and the types of information provided them. Thus, the memory situations encountered by children at home are numerous and young children do remember a great deal.

It is important, however, to keep in mind that these children were still limited in the types of memory abilities they displayed. The memory processing of young preschool children has been described as nonstrategic, nonplanful, and nondeliberate (Myers and Perlmutter, 1978) and the results of this study have shown that these earlier descriptions seem largely accurate. Memory functioning did not appear to be greatly controlled by children even in more meaningful and familiar settings. Young children in this study may have demonstrated that they are asked to and can remember information for relatively longer periods of time than have been shown previously; however, they appeared to retrieve information with difficulty and to do little to help themselves remember during the retrieval process. Conversations between mother and child concentrated heavily on here-and-now aspects of the world with mothers questioning relatively infrequently about past events and children recalling the past sporadically at best. Mothers were not frequently observed demonstrating mnemonic techniques nor requiring the child to perform behaviors which would help him remember. Thus, it is not surprising that children do not display a rich repertoire of memory skills in the laboratory when memory behavior is difficult to observe at home during daily routines.

The opportunity to observe only what children do is one limitation of a wholly observational approach, since the limits of what children can do is not observed as in more structured experimental settings. For example, children in this study spontaneously recalled relatively few events, an average of 7.2 when both age groups are combined, in conversation with their mothers, whereas Todd and Perlmutter (this volume) report that children of approximately the same age were recalling an average of twenty-five events when talking with an experimenter. The discrepancy may be due to the fact that while mothers do not typically engage in conversation to elicit memory episodes, Todd and Perlmutter did. When people unfamiliar to children or people they do not see regularly interact with them, I suspect as well that conversation revolves more often around past events and object information. In this situation the adult is not interested in directing or monitoring the child's activities and does not wish to test or teach the child. The goal is to maintain social conversation which largely involves discussing past events and talking about objects the child may share with the adult. Although I discouraged interactions between myself and the children I observed, there were times that I was approached by the children. During these times children appeared to talk about the past with me more often then they did with their mothers. Thus the individual the child interacts with, the goals of the interaction, and available contextual cues may influence children's abilities or willingness to recall. This was formerly apparent in comparisons of remembering at home and in the laboratory. Only marginal consistency was found and then only for the older children. Therefore, information concerning both what children do and can do in various situations is essential to fully understand the child's memory abilities and may lead to very different conclusions about the child's functioning. The most promising research approach appears to be one that combines observational and experimental techniques allowing control of variables in a systematic fashion and establishing cause and effect relationships, while providing descriptions of the behavior investigated.

This study has also tried to evaluate theoretical notions about memory based upon the Soviet view of its development. Vygotsky and those who have adopted his perspective have emphasized the importance of demands made in the context of social interactions and the functioning of cognition on an interpsychological level (between two people such as mother and child) previous to an intrapsychological one (autonomous cognitive functioning). Frequent memory demands were found in social interactions and were related to memory performance when children were three years of age. It was suggested that the child's activity involved in comprehending questions about past events and attempts to retrieve contextually bound information may be especially helpful in developing memory skills. Although relationships were found which supported the Soviet view that memory demands do aid memory functioning, these data were merely suggestive. Furthermore, it is not yet clear how demands facilitate development, if at all, nor how the child moves from joint memory processing with another to independent functioning. These issues must await future research.

References

Appel, L. F., Cooper, R. B., McCarell, N., Sims-Knight, J., and Flavell, J. "The Development of the Distinction Between Perceiving and Memorizing." *Child Development*, 1972, *43*, 1365–1381.

Atkinson, R., and Shiffrin, R. "Human Memory: A Proposed System and Its Control Processes." In K. Spence and J. Spence (Eds.), *The Psychology of Learning and Motivation.* Vol. 2. New York: Academic Press, 1968.

Brown, A. "The Development of Memory: Knowing, Knowing About Knowing, and Knowing How To Know." In H. Reese (Ed.), *Advances in Child Development and Behavior.* Vol. 10. New York: Academic Press, 1975.

Brown, A., and Scott, M. "Recognition Memory for Pictures in Preschool Children." *Journal of Experimental Child Psychology,* 1971, *11,* 401–412.

Chi, M. "Knowledge Structures and Memory Development." In R. Seigler (Ed.), *Children's Thinking: What Develops?* Hillsdale, N.J.: Erlbaum, 1978.

Cole, M., and Scribner, S. "Cross-Cultural Studies of Memory and Cognition." In R. Kail and J. Hagen (Eds.), *Perspectives on the Development of Memory and Cognition.* Hillsdale, N.J.: Erlbaum, 1977.

Corsini, D., Jacobus, K., and Leonard, S. "Recognition Memory of Preschool Children for Pictures and Words." *Psychonomic Science,* 1969, *16,* 192–193.

Crosby, F. "Early Discourse Agreement." *Journal of Child Language,* 1976, *3,* 125–126.

Cross, T. "Mother's Speech Adjustments: The Contribution of Selected Child Listener Variables." In C. Snow and C. Ferguson (Eds.), *Talking to Children: Language Input and Acquisition.* Cambridge, England: Cambridge University Press, 1977.

Daehler, M., and O'Connor, M. "Recognition Memory for Objects in Very Young Children." *Journal of Experimental Child Psychology,* 1980, *29,* 306–321.

Ervin-Tripp, S. "Discourse Agreement: How Children Answer Questions." In J. R. Hayes (Ed.), *Cognition and the Development of Language.* New York: Wiley, 1970.

Ervin-Tripp, S. "Is Sybil There? The Structure of Some American English Directives." *Language in Society,* 1976, *5,* 25–66.

Ervin-Tripp, S. "Some Features of Early Child-Adult Dialogues." *Language in Society,* 1978, *7,* 357–373.

Flavell, J. "Developmental Studies of Mediated Memory." In H. Reese and L. Lipsett (Eds.), *Advances in Child Development and Behavior.* Vol. 5. New York: Academic Press, 1970.

Flavell, J. "Metacognition and Cognitive Monitoring: A New Area of Cognitive-Developmental Inquiry." *American Psychologist,* 1979, *34,* 906–911.

Flavell, J., and Wellman, H. "Metamemory." In R. Kail and J. Hagen (Eds.), *Perspectives on the Development of Memory and Cognition.* Hillsdale, N.J.: Erlbaum, 1977.

Goldberg, S., Perlmutter, M., and Myers, N. "Recall of Related and Unrelated Lists by Two-Year-Olds." *Journal of Experimental Child Psychology,* 1974, *18,* 1–8.

Hagen, J., Jongeward, R., and Kail, R. "Cognitive Perspectives on the Development of Memory." In H. Reese (Ed.), *Advances in Child Development and Behavior.* Vol. 10. New York: Academic Press, 1975.

Holzman, M. "The Use of Interrogative Forms in the Verbal Interaction of Three Mothers and Their Children." *Journal of Psycholinguistic Research,* 1972, *1,* 311–335.

Horgan, D. "How to Answer Questions When You've Got Nothing to Say." *Journal of Child Language,* 1978, *5,* 159–165.

Horn, H., and Myers, N. "Memory for Location and Picture Cues at Ages Two and Three." *Child Development,* 1978, *49,* 845–856.

Hunter, W. "Delayed Reaction in Animals and Children." *Animal Behavior Monographs,* 1913, *2,* 1–86.

Hutt, S., and Hutt, C. *Direct Observation and Measurement of Behavior.* Springfield, Ill.: Thomas, 1970.

Kagan, J., Klein, R., Finley, G., Rogoff, B., and Nolan, E. "A Cross-Cultural Study of Cognitive Development." *Monographs of the Society for Research in Child Development,* 1979, *44, Serial no. 180.*

Kail, R., and Hagen, J. (Eds.). *Perspectives on the Development of Memory and Cognition.* Hillsdale, N.J.: Erlbaum, 1977.

Kintsch, W. *Learning, Memory, and Conceptual Processes.* New York: Wiley, 1970.

Klatzky, R. *Human Memory: Structures and Processes.* San Francisco: W. H. Freeman, 1975.

Kosslyn, S. "The Representational-Development Hypothesis." In P. Ornstein (Ed.), *Memory Development in Children.* Hillsdale, N.J.: Erlbaum, 1978.

Leontiev, A., and Luria, A. "The Psychological Ideas of L. S. Vygotskii." In B. Wolman (Ed.), *Historical Roots of Contemporary Psychology.* New York: Harper & Row, 1968.

Meacham, J. "Soviet Investigations of Memory Development." In R. Kail and J. Hagen (Eds.), *Perspectives on the Development of Memory and Cognition.* Hillsdale, N.J.: Erlbaum, 1977.

Myers, N., and Perlmutter, M. "Memory in the Years from Two to Five." In P. Ornstein (Ed.), *Memory Development in Children.* Hillsdale, N.J.: Erlbaum, 1978.

Neisser, U. *Cognition and Reality.* San Francisco: W. H. Freeman, 1976.

Newport, E., Gleitman, H., and Gleitman, L. "Mother I'd Rather Do It Myself: Some Effects and Non-Effects of Maternal Speech Style." In C. Snow and C. Ferguson (Eds.), *Talking To Children: Language Input and Acquisition.* Cambridge, England: Cambridge University Press, 1977.

Ornstein, P. (Ed.). *Memory Development in Children.* Hillsdale, N.J.: Erlbaum, 1978.

Paris, S. "The Development of Inference and Transformation as Memory Operations." In P. Ornstein (Ed.), *Memory Development in Children.* Hillsdale, N.J.: Erlbaum, 1978.

Perlmutter, M., and Myers, N. "A Developmental Study of Semantic Effects on Recognition Memory." *Journal of Experimental Child Psychology,* 1976, *22,* 438–453.

Perlmutter, M., and Myers, N. "Development of Recall in Two- to Four-Year-Old Children." *Developmental Psychology,* 1979, *15,* 73–83.

Rossi, S., and Wittrock, M. "Developmental Shifts in Verbal Recall Between Mental Ages Two and Five." *Child Development*, 1971, *42*, 333–338.

Sharp, D., Cole, M., and Lave, C. "Education and Cognitive Development: The Evidence from Experimental Research." *Monographs of the Society for Research in Child Development*, 1979, *44*, Serial no. 180.

Smirnov, A., and Zinchenko, P. "Problems in the Psychology of Memory." In M. Cole and I. Maltzman (Eds.), *A Handbook of Contemporary Soviet Psychology*. New York: Basic Books, 1969.

Snow, C., Arlman-Rupp, A., Hassing, Y., Jobse, J., Joosten, J., and Vorster, J. "Mothers' Speech in Three Social Classes." *Journal of Psycholinguistic Research*, 1976, *5*, 1–20.

Stevenson, H., Parker, T., Wilkinson, A., Bonnevaux, B., and Gonzalez, M. "Schooling, Environment, and Cognitive Development." *Monographs of the Society for Research in Child Development*, 1978, *43*, Serial no. 178.

Tulving, E., and Thomson, D. "Encoding Specificity and Retrieval Processes in Episodic Memory." *Psychological Review*, 1973, *80*, 352–373.

Vygotsky, L. *Mind in Society*. M. Cole, V. John-Steiner, S. Scribner, and E. Souberman (Eds.). Cambridge, Mass.: Harvard University Press, 1978.

Wagner, D. "The Development of Short-Term and Incidental Memory: A Cross-Cultural Study." *Child Development*, 1974, *45*, 389–396.

Wagner, D. "Memories of Morocco: The Influence of Age, Schooling, and Environment on Memory." *Cognitive Psychology*, 1978, *10*, 1–28.

Watkins, M., and Tulving, E. "Episodic Memory: When Recognition Fails." *Journal of Experimental Psychology: General*, 1975, *1*, 5–29.

Wertsch, J. "From Social Interaction to Higher Psychological Processes: A Clarification and Application of Vygotsky's Theory." Unpublished manuscript, Northwestern University, 1978.

Wilkinson, A., Parker, T., and Stevenson, H. "Influence of School and Environment on Selective Memory." *Child Development*, 1979, *50*, 890–893.

Yendovitskaya, T. "Development of Memory." In A. Zaporozhets and D. Elkonin (Eds.), *The Psychology of Preschool Children*. Cambridge, Mass.: M.I.T. Press, 1971.

Hilary Horn Ratner has been an NIMH postdoctoral fellow at the University of Chicago since receiving her Ph.D. degree from the University of Massachusetts in 1979.

The usefulness of current approaches to the study of memory and its development is discussed, and data are presented from a study that attempted to extend the focus of memory research using more naturalistic research techniques.

Reality Recalled by Preschool Children

Christine M. Todd
Marion Perlmutter

The purpose of this chapter is to provide information about the memory abilities of preschool children in relatively natural settings. Following a brief summary of what is currently known about memory functioning during this time period, the usefulness of current approaches to the study of memory and its development is discussed. Data are then presented from a study that attempted to extend the focus of memory research using techniques believed to be better suited to the study of very young children. The specific aims of the investigation were (1) to gain some understanding about the amount and type of information preschool children communicate to adults about past events in relatively natural situations, (2) to assess what elicits memory in the conventional format, (3) to get some idea of the time intervals over which young children retain information that is used in everyday conversations, and (4) to compare young children's performance on recall tasks that have different memory requirements. Following presentation of this research, the relevance of the findings to future research is discussed.

The authors would like to thank the families who participated in this study, and the research assistants who helped transcribe and code the data. The research was supported by a grant from NICHHD (No. HD11776) to Marion Perlmutter.

Current Research on Early Memory Development

Although much is still unknown about memory development in the early preschool years, a substantial body of research is available (see Perlmutter, 1980). To date, the study of young children's memory has focused primarily on deliberate memory for nonsocial stimuli over relatively short time intervals (seconds to minutes). The methodologies used to study early memory are almost exclusively cross-sectional and experimental and have tended to focus on group rather than individual data. Since emphasis has been on ascertaining underlying memory competence, the majority of studies have occurred in laboratory settings where control is most easily achieved. Response measures have been quantitative in nature, although in some cases qualitative aspects of the data (such as semantic clustering) also have been considered.

In general, the results of these laboratory studies indicate that very young children encode substantial amounts of stimulus information (Daehler and Bukatko, 1977; Perlmutter and Myers, 1974), although they do so more slowly (Morrison, Holmes, and Haith, 1974; Sheingold, 1973) and are limited by ineffective attention and search (Perlmutter, Hazen, Mitchell, Grady, Cavanaugh, and Flook, in press; Vliestra, 1978). The few studies that have dealt with retention of information over somewhat longer time intervals suggest that changes in this ability account for less of the observed developmental improvement in performance than do changes in retrieval skills (Brown and Campione, 1972; Daehler and Bukatko, 1977). Very young children appear to have substantial difficulty in retrieving information upon demand and do not deliberately make extensive use of semantic information to organize encoding or retrieval (Perlmutter and Myers, 1979; Sophian and Hagen, 1978). Furthermore, there is little evidence that preschool children engage in rehearsal (Perlmutter and Myers, 1979), and the retrieval strategies they use appear very primitive (Altom and Weil, 1977; Ceci and Howe, 1978).

Whereas research to date has provided substantial understanding of certain aspects of memory, investigations have centered on a narrow substratum of memory functioning, ignoring many other aspects that appear to be of equal interest. This fact is probably the result of an overreliance on a restricted set of paradigms. In general, developmentalists have been greatly influenced by experimental psychologists, often adopting their questions and methodologies. Unfortunately, it is not clear that the issues of interest to experimental psychologists should be of equal interest to developmental investigators. For example, while experimentalists most often have studied deliberate memory, this type of memory rarely appears to be encountered by very young children in their natural environment. Yet, there is little information about nondeliberate memory functioning, which is probably more central to young children. In addition, in the majority of studies, pictures and objects have been used as stimuli. With the exception of work by Nelson (1978), there has been almost no research on memory for social situations and activities. Finally, in most studies short-term retention of information is investigated. However, the everyday demands of learning a language and acquiring acceptable social skills almost surely require retention over moderate to long periods of time.

To understand memory in a broader sense, it will be essential to extend the factors considered and the types of information obtained. This endeavor will require new methodologies and analyses. Current methodologies often are lacking in ecological validity, especially when used with very young children. Furthermore, controlled experimentation can provide little information about certain important aspects of memory functioning, such as spontaneous retrieval of information, functions of memory in everyday life, and other more qualitative aspects of performance. In addition, the memory demands placed on young children in their everyday lives and the ways in which they use memory in the natural environment must be assessed. The past focus on memory performance in isolation from the natural environment, together with the lack of longitudinal data, have hindered our ability to ascertain the factors responsible for memory development. We have some idea of what develops, but almost no idea of the causes of that development.

Alternative Approach to the Study of Memory Development

The fields of ethology and language development are relevant to considerations of new methods for studying early memory development. An ethological perspective encourages one to study a broad range of behavior within a theoretical framework that aids in selection of specific areas of investigation. This approach requires careful observation and systematic documentation of behavior in the natural environment, as well as consideration of the adaptive function of behavior (or cognition) at various points in development (Lehner, 1979). While experimental investigations are required to test hypotheses and establish causation, initial stages of ethological investigations are descriptive in nature and result in categorizations that often are obtained through induction. Only after a phenomenon has been documented carefully can one begin the more controlled experimentation required to establish causation. Consideration of the adaptive function of a phenomenon is used to guide researchers in the initial selection of appropriate questions and remains important throughout the entire investigation.

The study of language acquisition offers another rich source of information about the study of early cognition. Similar to the study of memory development, the study of language acquisition involves inferences about internal processes derived through examination of observable behavior. However, language researchers have avoided many of the shortcomings of memory research through extensive use of naturalistic techniques and a concern for studying areas that have a fairly direct relevance to real-world functioning. Still, the tendency to use very few subjects has hampered attempts to discern the universal properties of language acquisition. In addition, the field has been criticized for its failure to establish links between factors identified as potential causes of development and the changes observed (Shatz, in press). It is for reasons such as these that controlled experimentation is used as well.

In considering the domains of both language and memory research the evidence suggests that an overreliance on a particular method of investigation, be it naturalistic or experimental, is unproductive. These two methods complement each other and an interplay between them is necessary for complete understanding of any question of interest. Both ethological theory and the relative success of work on language development suggest, however, that a progression from relatively naturalistic to more controlled techniques may be advantageous. Understanding of the organism in the natural environment is useful for establishing important issues for future investigation. It is this step that virtually has been ignored in memory research and that undoubtedly is responsible, at least in part, for the limitations of our present knowledge.

Naturalistic Study

In designing the study reported here, an attempt was made to obtain information that would complement and extend knowledge of early memory development. In contrast to highly controlled experiments conducted in unfamiliar settings, the present study was carried out in children's homes under relatively natural conditions. One of the advantages of this approach was that it permitted a fairly direct assessment of the effects of contextual support on memory performance. In addition, whereas standard memory tasks have been used to study primarily deliberate memory for nonsocial stimuli, incidental memory for both social and nonsocial aspects of past events was of central concern in this study. However, some information about deliberate memory performance was also obtained, so as to allow comparison of the children's abilities on the two different tasks. Moreover, long-term rather than short-term retention was of primary interest. Finally, while standard memory tasks preclude investigation of spontaneously retrieved information, in the present study possible differences in children's self- versus other-initiated retrieval was compared.

Method. The sample consisted of five male and seven female children from primarily well-educated, middle class families. Eleven of the children had at least one older sibling; one child had no siblings. The six younger children ranged in age from two-years, eleven-months to three-years, two-months (mean age = three years). The six older children ranged in age from three-years, nine-months to four-years, six months (mean age = four-years, two-months).

A female experimenter recorded two one-hour play sessions with each of the children over the course of approximately one month. An additional hour of conversation taped between the parent and child was used to provide a sample of normal speech. The mean length of utterances (MLUs) from the parent-child conversation ranged from 2.90 to 4.65 (mean = 3.72) for the younger children and from 4.19 to 6.20 (mean = 4.97) for the older children.

The play sessions were unstructured in that the children were not required to participate in any preplanned activity. The experimenter provided a few toys, but often the children preferred to play with their own toys. Over the course of the play sessions, the experimenter attempted to elicit children's remembrances by asking questions such as "Have you ever been to the zoo?" and "What did you do at school today?" Questions were asked when they were appropriate to the topic of conversation or situation. A conscious effort was made to avoid a rather strained question/answer format. In addition, each child was taught a game that required rote memorization of a short phrase.

Tape recordings of the sessions were transcribed and then returned to the parents who were asked to comment on the memory episodes. For two younger and two older children the parents were asked to comment on whether and when the events occurred, and the validity of the child's statements. For the other children additional information was obtained in a more standardized manner. Apparent memory episodes were marked on the transcript and the parents were asked to provide information about whether they recalled the event, when and where the event occurred, the accuracy of the child's statements, how often the child or parents had spoken of the event previously, and a variety of ratings concerning the confidence of the parents in responding to these questions.

Results. The findings are discussed in three main sections. First, information from memory communicated by the children is classified. Second, only nondeliberate memory for specific events is considered. Within this section, the amount, content, elicitors, and accuracy of specific information related by the children are discussed, as are prior rehearsal and retention intervals. Third, information about performance on a deliberate memory task is provided.

Types of Memory. The first major task was to isolate the instances of memory and to classify them. It soon became obvious that a simple classification such as episodic or semantic knowledge was insufficient for describing the complex ways in which young children were able to communicate information acquired in the past. In order to describe more fully the types of information found in the transcripts it was necessary to consider three factors: (1) the amount of detail communicated by the child, (2) the number of times a particular type of episode had been experienced, and (3) the duration of the episode (narrow versus extended time intervals). Table 1 portrays this classification system as well as examples of each type of memory episode.

The first major division concerns the level of detail provided by the child. It was surprising to find that even very young children, with limited commands of language, were able to communicate information that contained very specific as well as abstract statements. It was possible to divide up the episodes into three fairly distinct categories along this dimension. First, children

Table 1. Examples of Each Type of Memory Episode

Number of Occurrences	Duration	Level of Details		
		Specific	*General*	*Abstract*
Single	Single Point in Time	I went to John's house and played with a truck with 8 wheels.	John has a truck with 8 wheels.	Trucks can have 8 wheels.
	Extended Period of Time	I stayed at John's house for 2 weeks and we visited an interesting museum and went out to dinner.	John has an interesting museum in his town.	Museums are interesting.
Multiple	Single Point in Time	Once I went to the zoo and saw a bear sleeping and the next time I went it was eating.	Sometimes I go to the zoo and see bears.	Zoos have bears.
	Extended Period of Time	One Christmas we spent 2 weeks with Grandma Jean and the next Christmas we stayed with Grandma Mary.	We often visit relatives at Christmas.	Christmas is a time to visit relatives.

often related information about an event that had occurred at a specific point or series of specific points in time. In relating this type of information, the children used the past tense and provided information concerning the actions of themselves, others, or objects in a particular context localized in time. For example, a three-year-old spontaneously related the following information about a movie seen two weeks earlier. "And I saw movie too. It was Sleeping Beauty. And there was a icky witch . . . I was so tired I had even been sleeped in Mom's lap." As confirmed by the child's mother this event was localized in time; the child was communicating specific information about his own perceptions and actions at that time.

Children also frequently communicated information of a more general nature, which was characterized by the use of the present tense and a dissociation from a particular point in time. Some examples of such general statements were "G. has a fireman. We go to his house," and "Sometimes I go to the bakery." It often appeared that the children were providing a general statement that could have been derived from summation over a number of specific events of a similar nature. However, in a few cases the parents reported that the general statements referred to a single event.

Finally, there were instances of children communicating information of a highly abstract nature that was not directly related to particular events. For example, a three-year-old, while looking at a piece of corn he had found and explaining the circumstances by which it had been obtained, said "It's animal corn. No guys can eat it." In another session, a four-year-old spontaneously drew a circle in the air with his hand followed by a more meandering movement and stated, "This is round, and this is around." The first example is especially interesting because the statement was made while relating information about a specific event (going with a grandparent to pick the corn). The statement may represent something said to the child by the grandparent, and yet it was communicated to the experimenter stripped of its direct connection to the specific event.

In summary, there appears to be a dimension of communication from specific to general to abstract that is characterized by a progressive removal of context and dissociation from specific time referents. The children appeared very flexible in their ability to shift from level to level and within a single episode one might find a combination of specific, general, and abstract sentences concerning a common theme. It should be noted that these findings represent levels of communication and may not reflect underlying memory representations. It was not possible to determine whether the child who related general and abstract information was drawing upon a mental representation that was also general or abstract in nature, or was relying on specific knowledge but communicating it in a more general or abstract way.

The second dimension along which episodes were classified was frequency of past occurrence. It is possible to experience a particular event only once or more frequently. For example, one of the questions asked of the children was whether they had ever flown in an airplane. Some children had never flown, others had flown once or twice, and one had flown several times. This dimension interacts with levels of detail to produce a number of ways in which information may be discussed. For example, the child who had flown several times related specific information about several different flights. However, in relating the information she did not communicate that various aspects of the information had, in fact, occurred at different points in time. It is not clear whether this occurred because she did not separate the information into distinct episodes in memory or merely because the conversation did not require her to locate the information in time. In general, relating information about a combination of specific past events was done fairly often by both three- and four-year-olds. In some instances children clearly indicated that the events were separate, while in others they did not.

The last dimension along which episodes were classified pertains to the duration of the episodes. Some events, such as a trip to the zoo, are fairly continuous in nature and occur over a narrow time frame. Other events, such as

Christmas, can be more discontinuous and of a longer duration. For example, Christmas may include a number of activities that are separated in time, such as buying a Christmas tree, decorating it, visiting Santa, and opening presents on Christmas morning. Not everything that occurs between the beginning and end of Christmas is related to Christmas, as is usually the case with episodes of a shorter duration. In responding to questions about Christmas, children often spoke of a number of activities separated in time but all related to one particular Christmas season. In some cases, the older children also were able to provide specific information about more than one Christmas within the same conversation, although again they did not always indicate that the information pertained to different points in time.

The children's conversations contained specific information at each of the four levels of detail, although some categories were represented more frequently than others. It was less clear which of the four categories of general and abstract information was communicated. Unless an event had occurred only once, and the information provided could not have been inferred from other events, it was impossible to classify the episode unambiguously. There were, however, a few episodes in which the children communicated general or abstract information based on a single specific occurrence. For example, a three-year-old asked the experimenter to draw in the "sprockets" on the wheels while they were drawing a picture of a truck. The mother commented that she had discussed this with the child on only one occasion a few days earlier. This child appeared to be able to communicate and use information obtained from a single specific event in a more general way.

In summary, very young children appear able to communicate information resulting from single or multiple occurrences of events that can be long or short in duration. Furthermore, in conversations they can provide information that varies in the amount of context and time referents provided and are able to move easily from one level of communication to another.

Nondeliberate Memory for Specific Events. In order to gain some information concerning a single type of memory, those episodes in which the child communicated specific information about past events were investigated more thoroughly. For an episode to be included in this category the child had to provide detailed information about a specific or series of specific points in time and had to use terms such as "once," "a long time ago," or use the past tense. With only one of the youngest children (two-years, eleven-months) was there a serious problem concerning the ability to use the past tense. Parent reports were used to help classify these and other unclear episodes. The experimenter and an independent coder agreed on the selection of specific events with a reliability of .88

Amount of Specific Information. The results suggest that very young children are able to provide detailed information concerning a substantial number of specific past events. Over the course of two hours, children related information about an average of twenty-five past events (range = eighteen to forty-one), with the older children recalling slightly more episodes than the younger children (24.4 versus 21.5).

In order to assess the amount of information included in each episode, statements provided by the child were divided into memory units. One memory unit was assigned to each item of information concerning who and what was present, attributes such as size and color, statements concerning what occurred, locations, and temporal relations. In addition, one memory unit was assigned whenever a statement provided information about causation or the processes by which something occurred. For example, a statement such as "Mommy gave me a truck for my birthday" was assigned five memory units (two for the people mentioned, one for the object, one for the action of giving, and one for the temporal information provided). The experimenter and a second coder independently scored all episodes with a reliability of .83

The mean number of memory units recalled per event was 10.7, ranging from 5.6 to 15.0. Since the amount of information recalled could have been affected by experimenter questioning, the mean number of memory units per *wh*-question asked by the experimenter also was calculated for each child. This measure provides an index of the amount of information produced to each question. The children averaged 8.2 memory units per experimenter question, ranging from 2.9 to 16.0. While there was very little difference between the three- and four-year-olds in the number of memory units per episode (10.4 and 11.0), the younger children provided somewhat fewer memory units per experimenter question than the older children (7.6 and 9.6). Thus the younger children required somewhat more probing in order to communicate the same amount of information.

Content of Recollections. The episodes related by the children represented a wide variety of situations. Forty percent were about rather routine events, such as playing with toys, or interacting with parents or siblings. Forty-two percent were about events that were somewhat novel, such as a special event in a familiar environment (for example, a birthday or holiday) or a trip to a relatively new environment (such as a zoo, airport, or movie). The remaining 16 percent of the episodes were not easily classified along this dimension. There were no observed age differences in the type of information recalled.

In order to analyze information within episodes, memory units were classified according to their content. People who participated in events (21 percent), and what occurred during events (27 percent), accounted for about one-half of the memory units. Objects (13 percent) were specified somewhat less often than people and details comprised 17 percent of the memory units. Locative information (11 percent) was provided fairly often, whereas temporal information (5 percent) appeared less frequently. Abstract (4 percent) and causal information (2 percent) were seldom given.

It is possible that these proportions may have resulted from the types of questions asked by the experimenter. To check for this possibility, the memory units within each episode were categorized according to whether they were produced in response to an experimenter question or provided spontaneously. Approximately two-thirds of the memory units were provided spontaneously. The proportion of memory units in the above categories for spontaneous and elicited memory units were essentially the same, with the greatest magnitude of difference for any category only 7 percent.

The category of what occurred proved to be especially interesting. The statements within this category were classified according to who or what they pertained to. Seventy-seven percent of these memory units pertained to the subject or other people. Another 11 percent involved the actions of cartoon characters or animals. Only 12 percent of these memory units focused on objects. Thus the vast majority of statements concerned animate objects, primarily people. It also is interesting that the children did not confine their comments solely to their own role in past experiences. Twenty-seven percent of the memory units conveyed information about others and an additional 23 percent referred to both the child and others. Only about 26 percent of the statements pertained solely to the subject. A fairly similar pattern was obtained for both age groups. It therefore appears that even very young children encode and retain much information about other individuals.

The memory units concerning occurrences also were categorized according to whether they represented actions (60 percent); external states, including possession and stationary states (19 percent); sensory input (7 percent); internal states, such as emotions or cognitive acts (3 percent); or nonoccurrences (11 percent). The nonoccurrences category is of particular interest. Surprisingly, children not only discussed what had occurred, but also talked about what had not occurred. When relating information about a birthday party, for example, they listed who did not come as well as who did come. They often related that some family member had not gone with them on a particular trip. A three-year-old, when asked what happened when he went up the steps on an airplane answered "I didn't fall." In many cases these nonoccurrences seemed to represent a violation of expectancy. For example, since Daddy usually goes along with the family, those instances when this did not occur were significant. There appeared to be a progression with age toward providing fewer instances of nonoccurrences from 14 percent for the three-year-olds to 9 percent for the four-year-olds.

Another category for which there appeared to be age differences was internal states. Older children provided information about internal states in 4 percent of their statements, whereas younger children provided it only 1 percent of the time. This finding suggests that between three and four there is an increase in children's awareness of internal processes and states, or perhaps in their command of language relevant to these issues.

The interplay of memory and affect also was of interest. In order to obtain some information concerning the affective situation surrounding the events, two raters independently coded all episodes in terms of whether they felt the child was excited, happy, sad, angry, and/or afraid at the time of the event, and rated the level of excitement or affect as either low or high (medium was assigned in cases of disagreement). Fifty-three percent of the episodes seemed to show affective states that both raters agreed upon. The child was judged to be excited in 16 percent of all of the episodes, happy in 27 percent, afraid in 5 percent, sad in 3 percent, and angry in 1 percent. The level of affect was judged to be low in 14 percent of the episodes, medium in 20 percent, and high in 18 percent. There appeared to be few age differences in these findings, although there was a slight tendency for the younger children to report more positive and fewer negative episodes.

Elicitors of Memory. Approximately half of the memory episodes resulted from direct experimenter questioning. Forty-five percent of the remaining episodes were spontaneously retrieved by the younger children, as opposed to 56 percent for the older group. This difference does not appear to be attributable to a general hesitation on the part of younger children to communicate with a strange adult, since the younger children actually produced slightly more utterances during the two hours.

Eight percent of the episodes were child-initiated with no discernible external cue. Seventeen percent were cued by a physical object in the environment. In two-thirds of these episodes the child related information about the object itself, such as where it had come from or how it had become broken. In the remaining object-cued episodes, the child related information concerning a different but related object. Twenty-four percent of the episodes were cued by something in the conversation. The children were often cued by their own remarks. For example, a conversation concerning animals at the zoo led into an episode relating information about the circus, with animals apparently serving as a common tie between the events.

There was a tendency for the child-initiated episodes to reflect primarily routine events while the experimenter-initiated episodes more often dealt with novel occurrences. Sixty percent of the child-initiated episodes concerned common occurrences, as compared to only 36 percent for the experimenter-initiated episodes. It proved difficult for the experimenter to elicit comments about routine occurrences. Children did not respond well to general questions such as, "What did you do today?" or, "Where did you go with your mom this week?" At times it appeared that the children felt the experimenter already knew the answer to a probe concerning a routine event. For example, one four-year-old often responded by saying, "You know!" In other cases it appeared that the questions were formulated too vaguely to allow the child to select any particular topic for communication. Questions that referred to a very specific time or type of event generally were effective in eliciting information. For example, although questions such as "What did you do at school today?" typically produced answers such as "Nothing" or "Played," questions such as "What did you put on your Christmas tree?" or "Can you tell me one funny thing that happened at your school?" usually elicited information from memory. It therefore appears that very young children may require fairly specific direction in order to understand what is required or locate the appropriate information in memory.

Another interesting difference between child-initiated and experimenter-initiated episodes involved the amount of information provided to questions. While there was only a slight difference in total memory units per episode for the child-initiated and experimenter-initiated episodes (11.2 versus 10.1), there was a very large difference in the number of memory units given to experimenter questions in child-initiated versus experimenter-initiated episodes (13.5 and 5.4). The children provided more information per question about events for which they had initiated the retrieval process. This pattern occurred for both routine and very novel events.

Accuracy of Recollections. Parents provided information concerning accuracy for 80 percent of the episodes. Of the episodes rated, parents recalled the general event 79 percent of the time. For an additional 8 percent of the rated episodes, parents reported that it was quite likely that the event had occurred, although they had no direct knowledge of it. On the other hand, parents were confident that only 3 percent of the episodes had not occurred, and were unsure about an additional 10 percent. It also appeared that the detailed information contained within the episodes was quite accurate. For eight children, parents were asked to indicate whether or not the specific information contained in the episodes was completely accurate. Of the 63 percent of the episodes for which this information was provided, they indicated that 70 percent were completely accurate. There were no substantiated age differences in these analyses.

The errors made by the children were often interesting. For example, parents sometimes suggested that although the child was wrong, the error was probably in the perception of the event rather than in the memory of it. Failure to locate or convey time correctly was another common error. Several children had a general purpose phrase to indicate any past time, such as "the last day." Both three- and four-year-olds tended to express time in terms of some aspect of their own life or a major event, such as "when I was a little baby," or "at Christmas." In general, the three-year-olds seldom provided temporal information or used relational terms such as "first" and "then"; such information was provided somewhat more often by four-year-olds.

A better understanding of the true competence of young children to retain accurate information over long retention periods must await more controlled experimentation. However, the evidence again suggests that there may be fewer such differences between young children and adults than had been believed previously.

Prior Rehearsal of Episodes. One problem encountered in investigating long-term retention is a lack of knowledge about intervening rehearsal of the information occurring either covertly or during conversations with others. In order to gain at least some information about this factor, the parents of eight subjects were asked how often their children had talked about the episodes in the past. Parents responded to this question for 58 percent of the episodes. For 55 percent of these episodes, parents believed there had never been previous discussion of the episode, 22 percent had been discussed three or fewer times, 20 percent had been discussed over three times, and 3 percent had been discussed before, but the frequency was unknown. In several instances, the parents reported that the child had talked about the event soon after it had occurred, but not recently. There was only a slight difference between the age groups in the percentage of episodes discussed previously (41 percent and 48 percent for the three- and four-year-olds). However, there was a more substantial age difference in the amount of repetition of rehearsal episodes (52 percent had been repeated over three times by the four-year-olds, as compared to 35 percent by the three-year-olds). Thus, children appear to rehearse a substantial amount of memory information in conversations with others, and there may be a trend with age toward increased rehearsal.

One might hypothesize that discussions of episodes that had been repeated earlier would contain more information, since the conversations could serve both as a form of memory rehearsal and as a source of new information. The results appeared to support this hypothesis. Previously rehearsed episodes averaged 12.0 memory units per episode, versus 10.3 for unrehearsed episodes. However, for both younger and older children there appeared to be a curvilinear relationship between rehearsal and subsequent recall. Children seemed to benefit from some rehearsal, with the younger children benefiting more than the older. However, for both age groups extensive rehearsal resulted in a substantial decline in the amount of information communicated. The reasons for the observed decline are not clear, but may be related to boredom, hesitancy to communicate very familiar information, or the establishment of a core set of information that is accessed more readily.

Retention Intervals. Another question of interest was the length of time over which young children retained information. Parents were able to date 60 percent of all the episodes. In general, the majority of the datable episodes had occurred recently. Forty-nine percent had occurred during the month prior to testing, 17 percent one to three months earlier, 19 percent between three and six months, 12 percent between six and twelve months, and 3 percent over one year earlier. The accuracy of the memory units did not appear to change substantially with increased retention intervals. It thus appears that the children were able to retain information over relatively long periods of time with little decrease in accuracy.

There appeared to be age differences in long-term retention. The oldest event recalled by each child (that the parent was very confident about) had been retained an average of 7.7 months for the younger children and 14.5 months for the older children, with the age of the child at the time of the oldest event averaging 28.5 and 35.0 months for the younger and older children, respectively. Thus, although the older children were able to retain information almost twice as long as the younger children, their oldest memories dated from a later age.

The ability of these children to retain information from such an early age was impressive, and was corroborated by information from another of our studies. For example, the parents of one of the three-year-olds reported that while watching a commercial that displayed a bottle of honey, the child said she had liked the chocolate stuff her mother used to give her but not the yellow. The mother felt this could only refer to the chocolate syrup and honey she used to put in the child's bottle when she was a baby. The bottle had been taken away from the child at fourteen months. A similar experience was reported by parents of a two-year-old who, while looking at a picture of Santa Claus, remembered putting Sesame Street ornaments on the Christmas tree nine months earlier at the age of fifteen months. In both cases the parents were completely certain that the incident never had been discussed in the intervening time. These incidents appear particularly impressive since they demonstrate verbal recall of events that occurred prior to the time that the children were speaking extensively.

While memories of experiences dating back to two to three years of age can be obtained fairly routinely from young children, the two reported above were the only firm examples of memories pertaining to events occurring prior to two years of age. Two other children provided additional examples that may indicate memory for events that occurred in the second year of life but the details were too minimal for the parents to be sure.

Deliberate Memory in a Play Situation. In order to obtain information concerning performance on a rote memory task, each child was taught a novel rhyme. An object was chosen to represent a "bone" and the experimenter and child took turns hiding it while saying "Doggy, doggy, where's your bone? Somebody took it from your home." The other person then had to find where the bone was hidden.

The task proved very easy for the four-year-olds, requiring an average of four repetitions before the child was able to recite it perfectly or, in one case, with a substitution of only one word ("stole" for "took"). On the other hand, the three-year-olds found the task much more difficult. After four repetitions three of the younger children were able to provide an approximation that integrated parts of the two sentences, such as "Doggy, doggy, somebody took your bone from your home." The other three children were unable to give even a close approximation to the first sentence, producing utterances such as "Catch your bone" and "Doggy, you give me your bone." Two of the children in this latter group were followed over a period of three to four play sessions during each of which the game was played for a short period of time. These children greatly enjoyed the game and often wished to continue playing after the experimenter suggested they stop. Although they approached criterion, they were unable to produce a consistently correct response, even after they had heard the rhyme repeated twenty times.

The substantial difference in performance between the three- and four-year-olds on this deliberate memory task is in contrast to the assessments of nondeliberate memory, where only slight age differences were found. The results from this deliberate memory task are consistent with those obtained using free recall paradigms with children of this age. Since the children followed over a number of sessions appeared highly motivated and all of the children were tested in a familiar nonthreatening environment, it is difficult to attribute these results to situational factors. Furthermore, since the task was adopted directly from a nursery school setting and very young children know at least some nursery rhymes or songs by heart, it is difficult to argue that this type of task is completely invalid for children of this age. One might reasonably argue, however, that the task more truly represents a test of learning than of memory. When only material learned in a session was considered, both three-and four-year-olds showed similar high level retention over periods of several weeks.

Summary

The results indicate that under naturalistic conditions young children communicate extensive information about diverse past events. While a child's linguistic competence and range of experience undoubtedly affect memory performance to some extent, even children with very limited language abilities exhibit substantial recall. Furthermore, they are able to communicate information at various levels of abstraction and move freely from one level to another. This information appears quite accurate and sometimes has been retained over long time intervals. While young children are able to provide information concerning both novel and routine past events, when retrieval is self-initiated they relate information of a more routine nature and require substantially fewer probes to produce a given amount of information. Social encounters are particularly salient for young children and the memories communicated appear to refer to primarily neutral or positive events. Rehearsal of information acquired in the past is common during this age range. Limited rehearsal appears to facilitate recall, while extensive rehearsal seems to result in a decline in the amount of information communicated subsequently.

Age changes in nondeliberate memory seldom appeared as dramatic as those usually obtained in deliberate memory tasks. With age, children appeared to initiate more episodes and to communicate information with somewhat fewer probes. There was a slight tendency toward greater rehearsal of episodes with age. There also was a substantial age-related increase in the retention interval of the oldest events recalled, although the older children were unable to recall events from as early an age as the younger children.

In contrast to the relatively modest developmental change observed in nondeliberate memory, there appeared to be substantial improvements in deliberate memory abilities. Older children reached criterion in a deliberate memory task much faster than young children. However, both age groups retained information that had been learned for periods of several weeks with little decline in accuracy.

Implications for Future Research

The present study was designed to gain some understanding about young children's ability to communicate information acquired in the past. In addition, an attempt was made to ascertain the usefulness of a more naturalistic approach to research on memory. The method reported appears valuable for exploratory investigations. It offers the child much flexibility in response and yet affords some control to the experimenter. Moreover, because the children communicated information that they have chosen to store in memory, the data provide at least some understanding of everyday memory functioning during the preschool years. However, several limitations in this research approach must also be noted. The small sample size required by the scope of the investigation, together with the lack of independent verification of the statements made by the children and their parents, makes interpretation of findings tentative. Furthermore, while the results give some indication of the types of information young children store in memory, they are not adequate for evaluating how this information routinely is used or elicited in everyday situations.

References

Altom, M. W., and Weil, J. "Young Children's Use of Temporal and Spatial Order Information in Short-Term Memory." *Journal of Experimental Child Psychology*, 1977, *24*, 147–163.

Brown, A. L., and Campione, J. C. "Recognition Memory for Perceptually Similar Pictures in Preschool Children." *Journal of Experimental Psychology*, 1972, *95*, 55–62.

Ceci, S. J., and Howe, M. J. A. "Age-related Differences in Free Recall as a Function of Retrieval Flexibility." *Journal of Experimental Child Psychology*, 1978, *26*, 432–442.

Daehler, M. W., and Bukatto, D. "Recognition Memory for Pictures in Very Young Children: Evidence from Attentional Preferences Using a Continuous Presentation Procedure." *Child Development*, 1977, *48*, 693–696.

Lehner, P. N. *Handbook of Ethological Methods.* New York: Garland STPM Press, 1979.

Morrison, F. J., Holmes, D. L., and Haith, M. M. "A Developmental Study of the Effect of Familiarity on Short-Term Visual Memory." *Journal of Experimental Child Psychology*, 1974, *18*, 412–425.

Nelson, K. "How Children Represent Knowledge of Their World in and out of Language: A Preliminary Report." In R. S. Siegler (Ed.), *Children's Thinking: What Develops.* New York: Erlbaum, 1978.

Perlmutter, M. "Development of Memory in the Preschool Years." In R. Green and T. D. Yawkey (Eds.), *Early and Middle Childhood: Growth, Abuse, and Delinquency and Its Effects on Individual, Family, and Community.* Westport, Conn.: Technomic, 1980.

Perlmutter, M., Hazen, N., Mitchell, D. B., Grady, J. G., Cavanaugh, J. C., and Flook, J. P. "Picture Cues and Exhaustive Search Facilitate Very Young Children's Memory for Location." *Developmental Psychology*, in press.

Perlmutter, M., Myers, N. A. "Recognition Memory Development in Two- to Four-Year-Olds." *Developmental Psychology*, 1974, *3*, 447–450.

Perlmutter, M., and Myers, N. A. "Development of Recall in Two- to Four-Year-Old Children." *Developmental Psychology*, 1979, *15*, 73–83.

Shatz, M. "On Mechanisms of Language Acquisition: Can Features of the Communicative Environment Account for Development?" In L. Gleitman and E. Wanner (Eds.), *Language Acquisition: The State of the Art,* in press.

Sheingold, K. "Developmental Differences in Intake and Storage of Visual Information." *Journal of Experimental Child Psychology,* 1973, *16,* 1-11.

Sophian, C., and Hagen, J. W. "Involuntary Memory and the Development of Retrieval Skills in Young Children." *Journal of Experimental Child Psychology,* 1978, *26,* 458-471.

Vliestra, A. G. "The Effect of Strategy Training and Stimulus Saliency on Attention and Recognition in Preschoolers." *Journal of Experimental Child Psychology,* 1978, *25,* 17-32.

Christine M. Todd is a graduate student at the University of Minnesota's Institute of Child Development, where she is an NIMH graduate fellow.

Marion Perlmutter is an associate professor at the University of Minnesota's Institute of Child Development, where she has been on the faculty since receiving her Ph.D. degree in psychology from the University of Massachusetts in 1976.

An attempt is made to explain why patterns of recall differ between different age groups of young children.

The Generalities and Specifics of Long-Term Memory in Infants and Young Children

Katherine Nelson
Gail Ross

How is memory in the first three years of life related to memory in the older child or adult? This is a classic question raised originally by the phenomenon termed infantile amnesia by Freud and later Freudians. Adults and older children do not usually remember incidents from their lives that happen prior to the age of three. For most people the number of memories increases after the age of three and by the school years (seven or eight) becomes a flood of remembered episodes forming an autobiographical history.

This phenomenon has given rise to much speculation and theorizing, but little empirical research. The basic question is whether the lack of early memories implies that the memory system itself is different in the early years or whether other factors, such as changes in cognitive organization (or repression, as Freud, 1924, theorized) are responsible for the effect.

The research with two-year-olds reported in this chapter was carried out with support from the National Science Foundation (Grant No. BNS–78–25810) and from the Carnegie Corporation of New York.

To begin an empirical attack on this question, one needs to determine whether infants and young children remember events that they experience for any significant period of time. That is, is the amnesia truly a *loss* or is it simply a *lack*? Until recently there was little convincing evidence on this point.

Recent research (Fagan, 1973) has demonstrated that after a two-week delay infants as young as four and five months will recognize facial photographs that they have previously been exposed to for only one to two minutes. These experiments use a now common habituation paradigm in which the infant is exposed to a stimulus (in this case photographs) for a certain time period and is later tested with the familiar stimulus paired with a novel stimulus. Differential looking to the novel stimulus indicates recognition of the familiar one. This finding contrasts markedly with an early study of hospitalized infants of similar age (Lindquist, 1945) in which a limit of five days delay was found for the recognition of mother, surely a more salient and familiar stimulus to a baby than Fagan's photographs!

Types of Infant Memory

Elsewhere in this volume (Ashmead and Perlmutter) evidence is presented that shows not only recognition memory in seven-, nine-, and eleven-month-old infants over delays longer than two weeks but also evidence for recall memory at those ages. This evidence is important because it has been argued that an important difference between infants and adults is one of different types of memory, in particular the ability to recognize previously presented stimuli, but not to recall them spontaneously. This distinction demonstrates the importance of clarifying precisely what we mean by memory in the young child when relating it to later memory development.

It is quite clear that infants and toddlers are acquiring a large store of information about the world that they live in, and this knowledge is demonstrated daily in action, as the child anticipates familiar routines, recognizes familiar people, or plays familiar games. On one reading of memory, all this knowledge may be called memory. This reading would be similar to what Piaget (1973) calls memory in the broad sense, that is, memory for what has been learned, as opposed to memory in the narrow sense, memory for a specific event. Tulving (1972) termed such knowledge semantic memory (see Nelson and Brown, 1978), making a distinction between episodic memory, which is remembered in terms of a specific occasion, and semantic memory, including all known factual information. We will call this general memory or simply knowledge. In prior studies (Nelson, 1978; Nelson and Gruendel, 1979) we have presented evidence that in the young child this general knowledge base is organized in terms of general event structures, that is, in the form of knowledge of familiar routines (Nelson, 1978). Schank and Abelson (1977) claim that much of the adult's knowledge of the world is represented in similar form. To the extent that this is the case, one answer to the question raised at the outset is that the relation between infant memory and later memory is one of similarity of form — both reflect general knowledge of events, structured in similar ways.

However, on a different reading of memory, the evidence is less clear. In this more specific reading the question is framed in terms of memory in the strict sense (Piaget) or episodic memory (Tulving, 1972) or autobiographical memory (Schachtel, 1947). It is in this sense of memory that the issue of infantile amnesia arises, for it is the lack of memory of specific episodes prior to the age of about three that is so striking. The investigation of early childhood memory then is best formulated in terms of evidence for the existence of and properties of specific memory during this period. As we accumulate evidence with respect to memory we need to continuously ask, is this evidence of general knowledge or is it evidence that the child remembers a specific episode or occasion? Clearly, the evidence from habituation studies is evidence for only the former supposition, and most of the evidence that we have on the basis of anecdote and observation consists of children's knowledge of routine events, rather than of specific episodes.

At this point two related issues need to be raised. The first is the claim by Piaget that representation as such develops only toward the end of the sensorimoter period with the development of the symbolic function. This claim appears to make specific memory as we have been discussing it impossible prior to eighteen months to two years, regardless of the persuasive evidence for long-lasting recognition memory in infancy. In order to have and use memory (either general or specific) mental representation is apparently necessary.

This issue of representation is related to that of recognition versus recall, in that Piaget admits that the infant recognizes familiar objects and events, but maintains that he cannot re-present these to himself. Thus another way of stating the representational issue is to say (as was suggested earlier) that the infant possesses recognition memory but not recall memory. These then would provide two related answers to the question raised at the outset: infant memory differs from later memory in that infants lack mental representation, or, while they have recognition memory they do not have recall memory.

However, this position loses some force if one agrees with Spear (1978) that all memory is cued in some way and the only question is the nature of the cue and its connection to what is recalled. For example, children who recognize a bottle as an object to be sucked and bring their sensorimotor sucking schema into play when they see the bottle have established an association between the two such that recognition of one recalls the other (Piaget would say that the bottle is assimilated to the sucking schema). Our case would be stronger, however, if we could show that the sensorimotor schema of sucking cued a mental representation (that is, recalled the memory) or the bottle, since we do not claim that a motor act like sucking is represented mentally in the same sense as an object or event.

Thus far, we have considered different possible answers to the question of the relation between memory in the infant and toddler and in the older child and adult. In these considerations we have suggested ways that the memory system itself might differ at the early stage. In addition to those ways that we have considered, information processing in general is slower in the infant because of the immaturity of the central nervous system. This difference might in turn affect what can be processed from any given event and thus prevent the child from storing memories in such a way that they would be retrievable in a form that was usable at a later stage. The argument here is similar to Schachtel's (1947) suggestion of different organizing principles at different stages, making the knowledge from an early stage inaccessible to later probes.

Theories of Infantile Amnesia

Having reviewed the arguments for both similarity and differences between early and later memory, we need to consider theories that have been specifically addressed to the question of why infant memories—if they exist—are lost; that is, theories of infantile amnesia, and to show what research on early memory can contribute to improving these theories. It is sometimes asserted that the loss of early memories is a function of time, with the longer-held memories dropping out. It is easy to show, however, that this is incorrect in that the early childhood cutoff does not change importantly whether it is older children (eight to ten years) or adults who are being questioned. It cannot then be a function of time lapse but rather of an absolute age constraint.

Freudian theory proposes that early memories are not different in kind from later memories but are repressed in order to blot out memory of infantile sexuality with all of its threats to adult conventionality and rationality. The notion of "screen memories" is invoked to explain why so many early memories are not of emotionally charged material but rather of quite ordinary events. The "screen memory" is remembered instead of the more threatening memory that has been repressed. The claim that most early memories are of routine and emotionally neutral episodes has not been verified in the various studies done since (Dudycha and Dudycha, 1941). Schachtel's (1947) important reconsideration of the Freudian theme draws more heavily on the influence of cultural schemes and the conventionalization of thought processes as explanations for the loss of early memory. His description of an unrecapturable, curious, creative, and free early childhood that simply does not fit the categories of adult thought, draws also on Bartlett's (1932) notions of the schematization of memory and thought.

Many investigators have tried to examine variables thought to be relevant to the Freudian theory, especially the emotional content of early memory (see Dudycha and Dudycha, 1941 for a review of the early literature). More recently, White and Pillemer (1979) have formulated a theoretical explanation that is related to the Freudian one in that it postulates a basic reorganization of cognitive processes at around seven years as an explanation for the phenomenon. They propose in addition a neurological development basis for this reorganization and the influence of social schemas along the lines of Bartlett and Schachtel. Campbell and Spear (1972) also consider several types of neurological development that might explain the loss of infant memory. However, the neurological processes they are concerned with (increase in myelinization of the association areas of the cortex; growth of dendritic fibers) are well established before the period that White and Pillemer consider crucial. Thus, while there is no evidence against neurological factors playing an important role in the amnesic phenomenon, the precise nature and timing of these factors is unknown. Moreover, any neurological development must be tied to psychological processes if it is to have explanatory power, and this step has not been accomplished in this case.

One of the most pervasive of the explanations for infantile amnesia is that memories cannot be retrieved until they can be verbally encoded for retrieval, and since young children are not verbal they cannot remember events that they experience. This theory appears more powerful to those who can easily accept its premises that cognitive processes in general and memory in particular depend upon the operation of internalized speech and that children below the age of three or four are essentially without speech. Among developmental psychologists these premises are not readily accepted today, although both were more or less conventional wisdom twenty-five years ago. Piagetian thinking has influenced most developmentalists to believe that cognition may be quite independent of speech. And the intensive study of children's language development has demonstrated that they are quite capable of using language to communicate, categorize, inform, and learn, long before conventional school age.

In summary, we can say that many issues have been raised in the course of theoretical consideration of the problem of specific memories in early childhood over the years, but that there is still a dearth of empirical work that can settle these issues. While a number of lines of investigation could be followed, the one that has been most neglected and that seems most likely to have a payoff at this point is the direct study of what young children remember under what circumstances. As the various chapters in this volume attest, several different investigators have aimed in this direction using techniques from questioning children about their memories, to experimental establishment of memory, to mother's diary accounts of evidence for early memory. We will report here an investigation that we have undertaken employing the last of these techniques. The prime question we addressed was whether we could find evidence for memory for specific events prior to the time when the child established facility with language. Subsidiary questions were what the content of these memories might be and what cued them. Since we could not query children directly for this purpose we instructed mothers in the keeping of diary accounts.

Long-Term Memories of Toddlers

As noted above, there have been few standardized studies of young children's memories for naturally occurring events. This paucity seems to arise from several factors. First, it is difficult to reliably establish the occurrence of memories in children who are limited in their ability to talk. Gestures and actions can signal important memories, but only for the observer who is aware of their referents. Relatedly, evidence for memories, even when very clear, occurs infrequently and unpredictably during the child's day. Thus, it is only serendipitous if an investigator is present when memory of a naturally occurring situation arises.

In this study we used a method modeled on the study of early language development and concept formation, that is, the mother's diary record. We asked mothers to keep a written account of every indication of a memory from their children referring to incidents that had occurred at least one week prior to the child's recollection. Mothers were used as the primary observers because they spent the most time with their children and were most likely to know the referents for their children's memories.

While the use of diaries is obviously fruitful for recording behaviors which would otherwise be missed, this approach does present some methodological problems. First, there is the aspect of mother's motivation. While some mothers may dutifully keep account of each and every one of their child's memories, others may record memories only when they "have a chance" or decide to describe only the most "interesting" recollections. Thus, finding that one child's mother has recorded ten memories and another child's mother has recorded only five does not necessarily reflect the first child's greater memory. Second, the information recorded inevitably reflects subjective interpretation. While one mother may perceive her son's pointing to a roof as memory of the time a flock of birds perched there, another may interpret that gesture merely as an indication of interest in the roof. Unfortunately, the reliability of mothers' accounts cannot be obtained, since they are in almost every case the only observer of the child's memories. Third, the type of information recorded about each memory may reflect the individual mother's focus. That is, some mothers may emphasize certain aspects of a memory (such as what triggered the child's memory), while others may attend more to other aspects (such as the amount the child can remember).

In this study, we attempted to gain some control over these variables by providing all mothers with the same set of instructions and training them to record memories in the same way, using several examples for standardized practice. In addition, we periodically reviewed our instructions and answered any questions they had about recording particular memories during the recording period.

Mothers of nineteen toddlers (10 girls and nine boys) participated in the study, keeping diaries of their child's memories over a three month period.

At the beginning of the study six children were twenty-one months old, six were twenty-four months old, and seven were twenty-seven months old. Each mother was given a diary with printed instructions and specific questions to answer for each memory. The second author explained the instructions in detail and helped each mother practice completing the information requisite for each memory. The following information was requested:

1. The time and date when the memory occurred.
2. The child's verbalizations or actions that provided evidence of the memory.
3. The circumstances—objects, people, situations, or verbalizations— that triggered the child's memory.
4. The time and date when the remembered object was last seen or the event last occurred.
5. A detailed description of the remembered object, person, situation, and so on and the context in which it occurred.
6. Whether the remembered object or episode was a novel (one-time) event or a recurrent one.
7. Whether there were any interim reminders of the remembered object or event. That is, had the remembered object or incident been discussed since its occurrence or had the child seen or been in a similar situation in the interim between the recalled event and its memory?

At the end of the three month period, mothers' diaries were collected and the data were coded. Each memory was classified in five different ways:

1. Kind of memory process in evidence: (a) recognition—naming or indicating knowledge of a specific member of a general class; (b) recall that involves naming or indicating knowledge of an object that is associated with a remembered object or situation; (c) recall that involves naming or indicating knowledge of some aspect of a remembered event.

2. Type of recall memory: (a) the location of an important person (for example, remembering in which house grandma lives); (b) the location of an important object (for example, remembering that raisins could be found in an aunt's kitchen cupboard); (c) an event or sequence of actions in a situation (such as remembering the plot of a movie seen by the child); (d) person/person, person/object, or object/object association (for example, remembering that medicine in the bathroom was taken by a cousin who was visiting); (e) a verbalization (such as remembering that Mommy *said* that Santa Claus puts toys under the Xmas tree); (f) absent object; that is, remembering that an object which was present in a particular place is no longer there.

3. Cue which triggered the child's memory: (a) sight of the object or person; (b) sight of the location; (c) verbal cue; (d) other sensory reminder (smell, sound, touch); (e) representation, such as a picture or photograph; (f) activity.

4. Novel versus recurrent memories.

5. Memories experienced directly by the child (such as eating a hamburger at MacDonald's or losing a water pistol in a Chinese restaurant) versus ones which were observed only (seeing Father mend a broken shelf or watching sister set the table). The interim between the occurrence of the remembered situation and the memory was also recorded. All memories were coded independently by both authors and disagreements were discussed and resolved.

Mothers recorded an average of 6.0 memories per child (range = three to fourteen memories), with twenty-one-month-olds having a mean of 5.2 memories; twenty-four-month-olds, 6.0 memories; and twenty-seven-month-olds, 6.7 memories. There appears to be little difference in the average number of memories recorded for each age group, but these numbers reflect mothers' recognition of children's memories and willingness to record them, as well as the actual number of memories which occurred. Whether there are any real age differences is unknown.

In the following analyses only the memories that reflected more than simple recognition of an object are considered (98 out of the total of 114).

Type of Memory. Forty percent of all the memories reported were ones in which children recalled some aspect of an event. For example, one boy, viewing photographs from his birthday party several months before, recalled that one of his friends broke a bus which had been a gift. A little girl who sat on the sidelines of her sister's dancing class showed that she recalled the dance steps that had been taught to her sister a week before. Of considerable interest is the finding that twenty-seven-month-olds were more likely to recall aspects of events than the younger children. The percentage of memories in this category for each age were: twenty-one months: 21 percent; twenty-four months: 35 percent; twenty-seven months: 53 percent. For example, one twenty-seven-month-old boy gave clear evidence of recalling the plot of a movie about a chemical which made animals grow bigger and then shrink. Seeing a glimpse of the movie on TV, he announced, "Dog get bigger, monkey get bigger, dog get smaller."

More common among the youngest group was the recall of the location of an important person or object. At twenty-one months 54 percent of the memories were of these types, at twenty-four months 35 percent, and at twenty-seven months 12 percent. Other types of memories (object-object or object-person association, verbalization, absent object) were recoded less frequently, although each occurred at every age, accounting for 25 percent at the youngest age, 29 percent and 34 percent at the two older ages respectively. A common memory for the location of an object among the youngest children was of receiving a lollipop from the bank teller at the drive-in bank. Either when passing the bank or driving into it, several children spontaneously said "Pop, pop."

In general, it appears that location of important objects is important for younger children, while episodes or events are more important to the older ones. However, it may also be that the greater speech abilities of twenty-seven-month-olds made it more likely that they would express knowledge about an event, while younger children, more limited in their productive speech, could only refer to single objects rather than the activities related to them.

Memory Cues. Eighty percent of all recalled memories were cued by the location where the object or event occurred (48 percent) or by seeing an object or person associated with the remembered object or event (32 percent). Recollections of twenty-one-month-olds, in particular, were cued by location (73 percent), while twenty-four- and twenty-seven-month-olds' memories were cued equally by location and associated person or object.

Memories triggered by other types of cues were interesting. Verbalizations by another person elicited 5 percent of the children's recollections. For example, one largely nonverbal child, hearing his mother say that she was going to make popcorn, moved his stool over to the stove so that he could watch the corn pop as he had done on a previous occasion. Other types of sensory cues also triggered occasional memories, as when a girl, waking from a nap, smelled brownies and called to her mother to ask if she was making brownies; or a boy, hearing a plane fly over his house, recalled seeing his parents off at the airport. Activity also triggered some memories (7 percent), as one girl's memory of Christmas caroling with her family was cued by their sitting around the piano singing folksongs. Viewing a picture or representation of an object or person triggered 7 percent of memories, primarily for the older children. Thus, for example, one twenty-seven-month-old girl, seeing a picture of King Kong on the cover of a magazine at the supermarket counter, recalled that she had seen a movie about him.

One striking finding of the study that may in the long run be significant is that there was no evidence from any report of a spontaneous (uncued) recall memory. In every case some recognizable external cue brought forth the verbalization or action that evidenced a memory.

Evidence of Memory. Evidence for the great majority of memories was verbal at each of the three ages. All recognition memories and all but three recalled memories were indicated by children's verbalizations about them, either alone or in combination with action. For example, a twenty-one-month-old girl, remembering the presence of a particular toy in her grandmother's sunporch, ran to the door of the sunporch, pointing and saying, "kitty" (one of the toys). Only a very small percentage of recollections (3 percent) were expressed through action alone, as in the corn popping example above.

The finding that children's verbalizations served as evidence of memory in almost all cases may merely reflect the fact that it is difficult to be sure that actions or gestures alone are indicators of memory for past events. Conservative interpretation by the mother may be a factor as well. Methodologically and theoretically this is a problem because the relation between language and memory is one of the factors of interest in the investigation.

Significantly, in this regard, we found, as did Todd and Perlmutter (this volume) a few instances of memories in which children were able to verbalize about events or objects they had experienced before they were able to label them. In one such case, a toddler who had moved away from his old neighborhood before being able to say the name of a friend who had lived down the block, clearly yelled the friend's name "Ar-wen-da, Ar-wen-da" (Arlen there) when he passed the house four and one half months later. Reports of this nature are evidence that memories can be stored and retained for several months, without reliance on a productive language system with which to retain them; and further, that language can later be superimposed on previously encoded preverbal memories.

Novel and Recurrent Memories. Information from the diaries showed that slightly more than half of the memories that were recorded were of situations, objects, people, and activities that were novel, that is, had occurred only once; while a little less than half were recurrent and had usually occurred with some frequency and regularity. There were no apparent age differences in these distributions.

Time Lag. Eighty percent of all memories were of objects or events that had occurred less than three months before (40 percent between one and four weeks before and another 40 percent between one and three months before). However, 13 percent of memories were of situations that occurred between three and six months before and 8 percent of situations that occurred between six months and a year previously. Twenty-seven-month olds remembered a larger number of objects and events beyond three months than twenty-one- and twenty-four-month-olds. The longest time lapse recorded was six months for the twenty-one- and twenty-four-month groups, and one year for the twenty-seven-month group. There appeared to be no relation between type of memory or cue and time over which it was retained. When temporal duration is examined in relation to novelty, it appears that novel as well as recurrent experiences lead equally to both long-term (over three months) and short-range (one month or less) memories.

In summary, we could characterize the relevant findings of this study as follows: Two-year-old children clearly remember experiences over long periods of time—up to one year in some cases. They remember things that happened only once as well as things that happened often. Although it appears that the memories of the youngest children center around objects and their locations, while older children appear to remember more about a total experience, this may only be a problem of the available evidence. It is easier for a child with limited verbalization ability to point to a location and say "cookie" than to recount something specific about the previous experience. It is striking that spatial locations figure so prominently in the youngest children's memories.

Comparison of General and Specific Memory in Preschoolers

Although this study showed that two-year-olds encode and remember aspects of their experience over a reasonably long time period, it could not, because of the verbal limitations of the children, verify whether their memories were specific autobiographical memories of the type defined initially or whether they were indistinguishable from general knowledge. The fact that a child remembers where things are kept on the basis of a single experience may simply indicate that he has entered that knowledge into his general script for use on the occasions when he is in that location.

Our previous research has indicated that children do have considerable *general* knowledge about recurrent events and that when asked to tell about familiar experiences, such as getting dressed, going grocery shopping, going to a restaurant or having a birthday party, they report such knowledge in a general form. For example, a very young child will say "You go there, you eat, and you go home." In pilot work carried out with three-year-olds, we had found, in contrast, that is was difficult to get these young children to remember specific events that had happened in the past. Linton (1979) reported a similar difficulty in her research with preschool children, when a request for a specific memory would often lead to a general account of "what usually happens."

We therefore undertook a study that attempted to contrast the general and specific memories of preschool children by asking on one occasion "what happens" when you have a snack at school or dinner at home and on another "what happened one time" (or "yesterday") when you had a snack or dinner. This question was followed by a question that asked the child to think about something special that had happened or to report what had happened on a field trip or at a birthday party that had been held at school.

Nineteen three-year-olds and nineteen five-year-olds took part in this study, carried out by Judy Hudson and Margo Morse at CUNY. The results of interest here are that, when asked to report on a specific episode, children were less able to do so than when they were asked about the general case. They reported significantly less information in response to the specific question. As in previous studies, we found that their responses to the general question were framed in general terms, that is, in particular, using the present tense. They used the past tense only for answering the specific question but they used the present tense also in this condition from 10 percent to 50 percent of the time. That is, they often slipped from past to present in the specific condition but rarely did the reverse — slip from present to past in the general condition.

In an attempt to determine whether there were qualitative differences in the content of the reports, the actions that the children reported were coded as either standard (typical of the usual situation) or particular (something likely to have happened only once or infrequently, thus to be a report of a particular instance). At both ages particular instances were much less frequent than standard (means of 7.5 and 1.6 respectively) and occurred four times as often in the specific condition as in the general, even though standard instances were much more frequently given even in the specific condition. Thus their memories appeared to be highly generalized.

When asked to report on something special that had happened to them, however, thirteen of seventeen three-year-olds and all but one five-year-old were able to reply (some children were not asked this question) and they gave relatively long and specific reports about such incidents as visiting the zoo, having a relative to dinner, and so on.

What these data seem to indicate is that, when asked about a recurrent familiar event, children remember it in terms of a familiar standard schema or script, although they are able to report specific memories about novel events as well. These specific memories included such things as building shelves with father, taking a trip, going to a museum, to the movies, to the ballet, beach, circus, or zoo. It is interesting that when they were queried about a specific birthday at school, however, they rarely gave specific information. It seems that novel events must be truly novel to be remembered in specific terms. School parties apparently were as routine as school snack time and could not be retrieved as specific episodes.

Making Sense of the Memory Data

In order to approach an answer to the issues raised in the introductory section of this chapter with respect to whether children's memories differ from or are similar to adults' and whether they are lost, repressed, or exist in different forms, let us formulate two possible courses of development. The first is a very familiar one. General knowledge is built up from the accumulation of many different specific episodes. At first, a particular experience will be remembered as a unique entry; if the person recalls it (or if the young child could recall it), it will be in the form of "what happened when I did thus and so . . . ." After a number of such experiences, the formulation would be generalized and the person would begin to speak of the general case, for example, "what happens" rather than "what happened." From this point of view, evidence for specific memory in infants and very young children shows the genesis of the accretion of general knowledge. The specific memories may be lost as the specific is entered into the more general knowledge system.

An alternative conception of memory development in the young child might propose that rather than accreting specific memories and finally generalizing to the general case, the child treats all experiences as examples of the general cases and does not code them as specific memories at all. Only after building up a strong general expectation about a familiar event within a familiar framework, including optional possibilities (dressing may be for play or for parties, for example) does the child finally come to the point of coding this place on this specific occasion, and even noting that certain options go together (for example, after breakfast teddy bear is likely to be found in the crib, whereas after lunch it is more likely that he will be in the stroller). The infantile amnesia phenomena can be interpreted within the latter framework by assuming that specific autobiographical memories cannot occur until there is a significant general base of event knowledge, which takes a number of years to build up.

What do the data that we have reported here have to say about these possibilities? The data from the two-year-olds shows that memories reported by mothers are about equally divided between novel and recurrent experiences. The data from three-year-olds show clearly that while both specific and general memory can be retrieved, general memories are easier to report for recurrent events. Thus there appears to be a kind of dominance of the general in young children's memory.

The data further suggest the following organization of memory in young children. It is spatially ordered and within a given spatial schema locations of people and objects are well located. It is probably also event ordered, organized in terms of scripts for familiar experiences, although for the youngest children the evidence here is more equivocal. Both novel and general memories are retained and are verbally retrievable on cue, even when they could not have been stored verbally. The general schema for a recurrent event is easier to retrieve and report than is a specific experience of that event although *novel* specific experiences can be reported on cue even by children below the age of two. Memories are not retrieved by young children in the absence of an external cue.

These findings suggest in turn a functional memory system in the very young child that differs in only a few specifics from that of the older child. Let us sketch here what seem to be the implications for memory development.

The memory system stores information about experiences. (Of course what will be stored from a given experience can be expected to change as the knowledge base grows more complex.) That information can be retrieved when another experience takes place that matches the first in some way; that is, when it is cued by a second experience. Under some conditions the second experience will be similar enough to the first to be considered a second instance of an event. Then the two will fuse into a common script for that event. When this happens, the individual instances will lose their identify and it will be difficult for the child to report specific memories about them. However, memories for single occurrences will retain a sharp identity and can be reported when cued by some familiar element, in particular a location or an activity.

With development it appears that two aspects of this system change. First, the child becomes able to retrieve single specific instances of routine events if they are distinguishable for some reason; that is, if they contain a salient differentiating element. Thus specific autobiographical memories emerge from the fusion of general schemas and scripts. Since most of the things the child experiences in early life are eventually repeated and thus do not remain novel, the one-time specific memories are likely to fuse with others over time. For example, Christmas is novel one year but recurrent the next. Indeed, the fusion process seems to be quite usual in young children's reports. Two different trips will be reported as one, for example.

Linton (1979) reports a similar phenomenon. She studied her own autobiographical memories over a period of years during adulthood, testing herself monthly on memories that she wrote down every day. Among her find-

ings was the fact that repeated experiences tend to blur together. A trip that was taken only once could be remembered but if she experienced two interviews at the same university or attended the same committee meetings over a number of years, then she had difficulty sorting the occasions out one from another. As she puts it, episodic memories diminished as semantic memory (general knowledge about the type of experience) increased. This discovery is highly consonant with the findings from our studies of children.

The ability to retrieve a differentiated instance of a recurrent event is thus one probable development. On the basis of our script studies it seems likely that this development takes place around the age of four or five as the child is able to report alternative choices in a given script — for example, the report by one child that you could wear a party dress if you were getting dressed for a wedding.

The other important development seems likely to be the ability to retrieve memories in the absence of external cues. This process is essential to independent thought and imaginative activities (perhaps also to representational art), as well as to the establishment of an autobiographical memory stream of one's own. One has to be able to say to a friend, "Do you remember when we built the playhouse?" as well as to respond to such questions. If our data are a valid representation of the situation, young children appear to be able to do the latter but not the former.

Thus the direction of memory development does not appear to us to be unidirectional but to proceed from single novel experiences to fused representations to differentiated representations that are capable of being recalled and shared in the absence of external cues. Prior to the achievement of the latter two steps, individual autobiographical memories will not be remembered as such. According to this analysis, the phenomenon of infantile amnesia is not a function of language or of reorganization of experience or the lack of memories or of repression but of normal processes of growth and development.

This is not to say that language may play no role in the development of the memory system. It may well be that the development of the internal retrieval process is facilitated by recounting and verbally sharing memories with others. Indeed, it seems probable that something of the sort is influencing the process when we consider the vast individual differences in autobiographical memory development.

These proposals suggest numerous lines for further investigation. Despite the necessarily informal methods employed in these studies, the answers to the questions raised are important and basic to our understanding of the cognitive functioning of young children. Further probing of memory in very young children is likely to reveal important insights that can be gained in no other way.

References

Bartlett, S. C. *Remembering: A Study in Experimental and Social Psychology.* Cambridge, England: Cambridge University Press, 1932.

Campbell, B. A., and Spear, N. E. "Ontogeny of Memory." *Psychological Review,* 1972, *79,* 215-236.

Dudycha, G. J., and Dudycha, M. M. "Childhood Memories: A Review of the Literature." *Psychological Bulletin,* 1941, *38,* 668–682.

Fagan, J. F., III. "Infants' Delayed Recognition, Memory, and Forgetting." *Journal of Experimental Child Psychology,* 1973, *16,* 424–450.

Freud, S. *A General Introduction to Psychoanalysis.* New York: Washington Square Press, 1924.

Lindquist, N. "Some Notes on Development of Memory During the First Years of Life." *ACTA Paediatric,* Stockholm, 1945, *32,* 592–598.

Linton, M. "Cuing Events in Adults' and Children's Autobiographical Memory." Paper presented at American Psychological Association meeting, New York, 1979.

Myers, N. A., and Perlmutter, M. "Memory in the Years from Two to Five." In P. A. Ornstein (Ed.), *Memory Development in Children.* Hillsdale, N.J.: Erlbaum, 1978.

Nelson, K. "How Young Children Represent Knowledge of Their World in and out of Language." In R. S. Siegler (Ed.), *Children's Thinking: What Develops?* Hillsdale, N.J.: Erlbaum, 1978.

Nelson, K., and Gruendel, J. "At Morning It's Lunchtime: A Scriptal View of Children's Dialogues." *Discourse Processes,* 1979, *2,* 73–94.

Piaget, J. *Memory and Intelligence.* New York: Basic Books, 1973.

Schachtel, E. G. "On Memory and Childhood Amnesia." *Psychiatry,* 1947, *10,* 1–26.

Schank, R., and Abelson, R. *Scripts, Plans, Goals, and Understanding.* Hillsdale, N.J.: Erlbaum, 1977.

Spear, N. E. *The Processing of Memories: Forgetting and Retention.* Hillsdale, N.J.: Erlbaum, 1978.

Tulving, E. "Episodic and Semantic Memory." In E. Tulving and W. Donaldson (Eds.), *Organization of Memory.* New York: Academic Press, 1972.

Waldfogel, S. "The Frequency and Affective Character of Childhood Amnesia." *Psychological Monographs,* 1948, *62* (4), 291.

White, S. H., and Pillemer, D. B. "Childhood Amnesia and the Development of a Socially Accessible Memory System." In J. F. Kihlstrom and F. J. Evans (Eds.), *Functional Disorders of Memory.* Hillsdale, N.J.: Erlbaum, 1979.

Katherine Nelson is professor of psychology and head of the Ph.D. Program in Developmental Psychology at the City University of New York. She was formerly associate professor at Yale University.

Gail Ross is a research associate in pediatrics and psychiatry at Cornell Medical School. She was formerly an associate in research at Yale University.

Index

New Directions Quarterly Sourcebooks

New Directions for Child Development is one of several distinct series of quarterly sourcebooks published by Jossey-Bass. The sourcebooks in each series are designed to serve both as *convenient compendiums* of the latest knowledge and practical experience on their topics and as *long-life reference tools*.

One-year, four-sourcebook subscriptions for each series cost $18 for individuals (when paid by personal check) and $30 for institutions, libraries, and agencies. Single copies of earlier sourcebooks are available at $6.95 each *prepaid* (or $7.95 each when *billed*).

A complete listing is given below of current and past sourcebooks in the *New Directions for Child Development* series. The titles and editors-in-chief of the other series are also listed. To subscribe, or to receive further information, write: New Directions Subscriptions, Jossey-Bass Inc., Publishers, 433 California Street, San Francisco, California 94104.

New Directions for College Learning Assistance
Kurt V. Lauridsen, Editor-in-Chief

New Directions for Community Colleges
Arthur M. Cohen, Editor-in-Chief
Florence B. Brawer, Associate Editor

New Directions for Continuing Education
Alan B. Knox, Editor-in-Chief

STATEMENT OF OWNERSHIP, MANAGEMENT, AND CIRCULATION
(Required by 39 U.S.C. 3685)

1. Title of Publication: New Directions for Child Development. A. Publication number: USPS 494-090. 2. Date of filing: September 29, 1980. 3. Frequency of issue: quarterly. A. Number of issues published annually: four. B. Annual subscription price: $30 institutions; $18 individuals. 4. Location of known office of publication: 433 California Street, San Francisco (San Francisco County), California 94104. 5. Location of the headquarters or general business offices of the publishers: 433 California Street, San Francisco (San Francisco County), California 94104. 6. Names and addresses of publisher, editor, and managing editor: publisher—Jossey-Bass Inc., Publishers, 433 California Street, San Francisco, California 94104; editor—William Damon, Department of Psychology, Clark University, Worcester, Mass. 01610; managing editor—William Henry, 433 California Street, San Francisco, California 94104. 7. Owner: Jossey-Bass Inc., Publishers, 433 California Street, San Francisco, California 94104. 8. Known bondholders, mortgages, and other security holders owning or holding 1 percent or more of total amount of bonds, mortgages, or other securities: same as No. 7. 10. Extent and nature of circulation: (Note: first number indicates the average number of copies of each issue during the preceding twelve months; the second number indicates the actual number of copies published nearest to filing date.) A. Total number of copies printed (net press run): 2513, 2537. B. Paid circulation, 1) Sales through dealers and carriers, street vendors, and counter sales: 85, 40. 2) Mail subscriptions: 594, 592. C. Total paid circulation: 679, 632. D. Free distribution by mail, carrier, or other means (samples, complimentary, and other free copies): 125, 125. E. Total distribution (sum of C and D): 804, 757. F. Copies not distributed, 1) Office use, left over, unaccounted, spoiled after printing: 1709, 1780. 2) Returns from news agents: 0, 0. G. Total (sum of E, F1, and 2—should equal net press run shown in A): 2513, 2537.

I certify that the statements made by me above are correct and complete.

JOHN R. WARD
Vice-President